180° South

Conquerors of the Useless

Patagonia Books

180° South

Conquerors of the Useless

copyright 2010 Patagonia Books

Text © Yvon Chouinard, Jeff Johnson, and Chris Malloy

First edition

Printed in China

Cover photos: (clockwise from upper left) Scott Soens, Lito Tejada-Flores, Scott Soens, Jeff Johnson

ISBN 978-0-9790659-4-1 (regular edition)
ISBN 978-0-9790659-8-9 (boxed edition)

The *Cahuelmo* anchored in an estuary. Below Cerro Corcovado, Patagonia, Chile. Photo: Scott Soens

One of the biggest social and environmental issues facing Chile is the damming of rivers. Local residents have started a campaign against the dams called ¡Sin Represas! (Without Dams). Money from Patagonia's sale of a poster and T-shirt (art shown here) will be donated to charitable organizations connected to !Sin Represas! Art: Shepard Fairey

TABLE OF CONTENTS

Photographs
Jeff Johnson, Lito Tejada-Flores, Scott Soens, Danny Moder, Jimmy Chin, Tyler Emmett,
Jeff Flindt, Devon Howard, Tom Servais, Chris Malloy, Jeff Divine, Grant Ellis, Chuck Pratt,
Hank Foto, Tom Frost, Chris Jones, Yvon Chouinard, Don James, Tim Davis, and Doug Tompkins

Illustrations
Shepard Fairey

Cover Font
Geoff McFetridge

FUN HOGS

YVON CHOUINARD

You never know how an adventure will influence the rest of your life. In 1968, when Doug Tompkins proposed that we drive from California to Patagonia – in those days a name as remote and alluring as Timbuktu – neither of us could know it would be the most important trip either of us would ever take. The goal was to put up a new route on an obscure tusk of granite called Cerro Fitz Roy and have some fun along the way. The experience led to an unlikely fate for a couple of dirtbags: we became philanthropists.

Doug owned a small outdoor store in San Francisco, where he had a few sleeping bags and tents sewn in the back room; I had a blacksmith shop in Ventura where we forged pitons and machined carabiners for a market that needed no research – we and our friends were the customers.

It took Doug and me only a couple of weeks to turn our work over to others, talk Dick Dorworth and Lito Tejada-Flores into driving down with us (English climber Chris Jones would hook up with us later), and secure a van – a high-mileage 1965 Ford Econoline. I built a sleeping platform in the back, and then we shoehorned in four pairs of skis, eight climbing ropes, racks of carabiners and pitons, camping gear, cold-weather clothing, warm-weather clothing, wetsuits, and fishing rods. We tied two surfboards on the roof. We took along the banner Doug's wife, Susie, made for us to fly from Fitz Roy's summit; its big block letters read "VIVA LOS FUN HOGS."

We all had complementary talents. Because I had taken auto mechanics in high school, I was appointed team mechanic. Doug and I were the most experienced climbers; Doug and Dick were expert skiers. I was a surfer, and Lito was a climber and photographer to whom we assigned the task of documenting the trip with a wind-up 16mm Bolex we bought secondhand. Lito had never before made a movie or even shot a movie camera. We were living up to Doug's credo, borrowed from Napoleon, "Commit first, then figure it out."

Only a week after leaving Ventura, we were surfing the breaks outside Mazatlán. South of Mexico City the pavement gave way to a dirt road that, except for a few concrete stretches through capital cities and a gap in Panama, would continue to Patagonia. Once we crossed into Guatemala, however, we confronted a challenge greater than a dirt highway. We were sleeping on the ground around the van when an army patrol woke us, a 16-year-old kid pointing his machine gun from my head to Dick's. We managed to convince them we weren't CIA agents, just tourists on a surf trip, then made a beeline for the border of Costa Rica, which had the only sane government in the region – and great surf breaks.

We had to scuttle our plan to stay there for a while when the volcano above our break erupted. So much ash fell between sets that the decks of our surfboards turned black – and it was almost impossible to breathe.

Yvon Chouinard aboard the *Cahuelmo*. Chaitén, Chile. Photo: Jeff Johnson

Tom Frost and Yvon Chouinard at the forge in the early years. Ventura, California. Photo: Patagonia Archives

We drove south to Panama to ride breaks that probably had never been surfed before, and then, to get around the roadless Darién Gap, drove our van onboard a Spanish freighter bound for Cartagena, Colombia. Dick, famous for his night driving skills – and aided by cassette tapes of Joplin, Dylan, and Hendrix, and a few other means – power-drove all the way to Ecuador, where I knew of a surf spot Mike Doyle had discovered.

All this time Lito filmed our adventure with the wind-up Bolex. Doug had talked me into sharing the costs of the camera and film with him. He was convinced that once home, we – the "producers" – could sell the film to make enough to pay for the trip and then some. (When we got back, we spent more money editing the footage into a one-hour film, *Mountain of Storms*, which made it into a few specialty film festivals but was never distributed.)

We surfed in Ecuador, then sold our boards in Peru. In Chile we pulled out the skis and skinned up and skied down Lliama, a big volcano outside Temuco, and farther south, Osorno, sometimes called the Fuji of South America.

Just south of Puerto Montt the highway came to an end, blocked by deep fjords and the great tidal glaciers descending from the continental icecaps. We loaded the van on small ferries and crossed sapphire-blue lakes framed by beech forests and snow-capped volcanoes, off-loaded the van, and drove the short distance to the next lake crossing. In Argentina, on the leeward side of the Andes, the landscape changed suddenly from temperate rain forest to open steppes, and the Econoline, seasoned by over 12,000 miles of hard driving, barreled down the celebrated Route 40, the dirt road that, on the Argentinean side of the Andes, connects northern to southern Patagonia.

Miles later we left Route 40 and followed a road more like a horse track around Lago Viedma, one of a series of large, glacially carved lakes in the southern Andes. This was the worst road any of us had encountered, and we didn't see another vehicle for 180 miles. Then the trail petered out entirely. In those years only a footbridge crossed the Rio de las Vueltas, so we parked the Econoline and talked some army soldiers into helping us carry our gear to base camp. The only other humans in the region were the gaucho Rojo, and the widow Sepulveda and her sons, who ran a sheep station three days by horse from Lago del Desierto.

At that point we had been on the road for nearly four months; it would take us another two months to climb Fitz Roy. The peak had been summited only twice, first by the iconoclastic Frenchman Lionel Terray, who wrote that Fitz Roy was one of two climbs he had no desire to repeat. Terray built his reputation on ascents of peaks that were obscure to laymen but considered classics by climbers for their beauty or the difficulty of their routes. He understood that how you reached the summit was more important than the feat itself. His approach appealed to those of us who had cut our teeth on first ascents of Yosemite's high walls, where you got to the top only to realize there wasn't anything there. Terray said it all when he titled his autobiography *Conquistadors of the Useless*.

Chouinard Equipment employees in 1966. Ventura, California. Photo: Tom Frost

Tools of the trade: hand-forged climbing gear made by Chouinard Equipment in the 1960s. Photo: Patagonia Archives

Once at the base of Fitz Roy, between brief breaks in the scudding clouds we could trace a line of ascent (now called the Ruta de los Californianos) that would be hard but doable. Then the weather changed.

Because the Andes rise so suddenly out of the Southern Ocean, the storms that blow in the latitudes of the Howling Fifties collide with the peaks like a train hitting a huge wall. The winds of Patagonia are so strong you feel you can bite into them.

Our tents were no match for such winds, so we had to dig snow caves, including one at the base of the final rock ridge leading to the summit that became our high camp. In the 60 days it took us to reach the summit, we had only five days of weather clear enough to climb. The rest of the time we waited.

I spent a total of 31 days confined to a snow cave. I had skewered my knee with my ice axe while cutting ice for the stove. So while the others left periodically to go down and rustle a sheep to augment our meager food reserves, I stayed on my back staring at a gloomy ceiling of ice melting inches above my face. Every time we started the stove to cook, the walls dripped onto our down sleeping bags, which became useless wet lumps. We were perpetually cold and hungry. I turned 30 years old inside that cave; it was a low point in my life. But because it honed me to handle adversity, it was a high point too.

When the weather finally broke, we knew we had to move fast. Doug and I led the pitches, and at the top of each we fixed a rope that Lito would then ascend to film us as we started the next pitch. Dick and Chris followed carrying our gear. We were very efficient, and before sunset we reached the top and posed while Lito filmed us holding Susie's banner.

The feeling of jubilation on the summit of any tough climb is tempered by the awareness that you still have to get down. We couldn't get back to the ice cave before dark, and after 21 hours straight of climbing and rappelling we were forced to bivouac. The wind returned and it was a miserable night, but as another climbing friend Doug Scott once said about a bivouac high on Everest, the quality of the survival was good.

- - - - -

Doug has said that spending so much of our formative years in close proximity to the beauty of nature allowed an appreciation for it to enter our bones. Appreciate something for long enough and you learn to love it. And anytime you love something, you also want to care for it and safeguard it.

In the mid '80s I returned to the base of Fitz Roy with my friends Rick Ridgeway and Tom Brokaw. At the roadhead we stepped out of our van to begin the trek: In the grassy fields, where only 15 years earlier Rojo's sheep grazed, lay a maze of survey markers, each with a pennant of orange tape marking the location of a new street, a new restaurant, a new hotel. A few months later the town of El Chaltén was under construction.

By then my business had grown. So had Doug's. While he was away on our long road trip, Susie started a small line of boutique women's dresses called Plain Jane that she and Doug later developed into a billion-dollar company called Esprit.

My wife, Malinda, and I also went into the rag trade, after importing some rugby shirts from Scotland that took off and threatened to make enough profit to support the climbing business. The clothes,

Doug Tompkins on the first ascent of Ruta de los Californianos in 1968. Cerro Fitz Roy, Chile. Photo: Chris Jones

Doug Tompkins during an expedition to the Trango Towers in the mid 1980s. Baltistan, Pakistan. Photo: Doug Tompkins Collection

like the gear, had to be strong, long lasting, and perform perfectly for the use intended. We introduced clean lines, bold colors, and light, technical layering to outdoor clothing – and named our new company Patagonia.

Doug and I wanted to give back to what we cared about most. By the mid-1980s Patagonia, the company, had started to give 1 percent of its sales to grassroots organizations to help save a patch of land here or a stretch of river there. Around the same time, recognizing the environmental damage business does, Esprit introduced its pioneer "eco-collection" of women's wear made with natural fibers and dyes and organically grown cotton.

In 1990, I decided to take the senior management of my company off-site for an examination of our goals and responsibilities. We loaded our backpacks, and Patagonia-the-company journeyed to Patagonia-the-place. The experience was seminal. Coming out of that trip, and during the sessions that followed our return, we wrote the company mission statement still used to guide our decisions: "Build the best product, cause no unnecessary harm, and use business to inspire and implement solutions to the environmental crisis."

A bit later on, we did an analysis of the environmental impacts of our four main clothing fibers. On learning that conventional cotton accounted for 25 percent of all the insecticides used in world agriculture, we decided to go organic – even though there wasn't enough organic cotton available then to supply our needs. In the early 2000s we introduced the first closed-loop recycling program in the clothing industry, and most recently we created a Web site where our customers can examine the environmental consequences of the clothing they buy from us, both the good and the bad.

During the past 20 years there have been a few times when, frustrated with the business, I've thought about selling it, putting the money into a foundation, and using it to effect environmental change and protection. Each time, though, I've decided that the better strategy was to keep the company and use it as a model for responsible business.

That wasn't true for Doug, however. In the late '80s, after he and Susie divorced, he sold his half of Esprit and put the money into his own foundation. At first he followed the same strategy we had at Patagonia, making grants to small, front-line environmental groups. But then he hatched a plan for an entirely different model. Land in Patagonia was cheap, but also threatened by construction – as we had seen with El Chaltén at the base of Fitz Roy – and by oil and gas development and overgrazing on the estancias. What if he used his foundation's resources to buy these threatened lands and protect them?

Doug flew his small Cessna to southern Chile and Argentina to check out estancias that might be for sale. He bought several parcels, including a farm on the edge of a fjord that would become home to him and his second wife, former Patagonia CEO Kristine McDivitt. He then began acquiring contiguous properties that he eventually would combine into Pumalín – at nearly 800,000 acres, the largest privately held park in the world.

Kris joined Doug in his work on conservation projects across Patagonia, including a new effort of her own called Conservación Patagónica. She wanted to attract the support of philanthropists to help acquire large properties that would then be returned to the people of Chile or Argentina. Her first project was on the Atlantic coast just north of the Straits of Magellan. Today Monte Leon is Argentina's first and only maritime national park, protecting 26 miles of wild coastline, home to a vital seal rookery as well as a penguin colony of about half a million birds. Her current project is to create Patagonia National Park, centered around the magnificent Valle Chacabuco that cuts transversally through the Andes, providing habitat for overlap species from both the wet windward as well as the dry leeward biomes.

This project is in a sense all in the family. Patagonia, the company, has contributed money as well as subsidized employees to do volunteer work removing fences and eradicating non-native plants.

Our company has become an attractive place to work for anyone who cares about the fate of the planet, and this in turn has made it easy to recruit good employees. It's also an appealing company to the outdoor athletes who test and promote our products. We attract some of the top climbers, surfers, and skiers in the world, not so much the most competitive, but those who relate to the soul of the sport – climbers who are more into the quality of the route than gaining the summit, and surfers more interested in an undiscovered wave on a remote coastline than another contest prize.

That is certainly the case with one of our key surf ambassadors, Chris Malloy. Before he decided to look me up, and then come to work for us, Chris began his own pilgrimage trying to understand his growing disillusionment with the life of a professional competitive surfer. He was living in Hawai'i, wrestling with those questions, when a close friend and North Shore lifeguard named Jeff Johnson showed him a copy of an obscure film about a bunch of friends back in the 1960s who bought a funky Ford van and drove it all the way from California to a place called Patagonia.

Chris and his friends were kind enough to include Doug and me in their revisit of our adventure – and to take advantage of some typically nonstop Patagonia rain to ply us with questions on how we came to value what we do and how we set down our road. The photos and stories in this book give you the perspectives of two generations of climbers and surfers who have come into contact with the wild and had their lives changed forever. It is the nature of nature that you can't come to know it from a book, but you can get a glimpse here. Even that much will make you want to act – and live for it.

Doug Tompkins and Billy Kidd taking time out from ski races in the early 1960s. Valparaiso, Chile. Photo: Doug Tompkins Collection

Doug Tompkins climbing in typical Scottish conditions in the early 1970s in the Cairngorms, Scotland. Photo: Yvon Chouinard

Tom Frost, Doug Tompkins, Dick Dorworth, Yvon Chouinard, and Lito Tejada-Flores in front of Chouinard Equipment prior to their 1968 road trip south to climb Cerro Fitz Roy.

Ventura, California. Photo: Patagonia Archives

In the late 1990s photographer and Patagonia employee Amy Kumler snuck the *Mountain of Storms* VHS tape from the Patagonia vault and gave it to Jeff Johnson to view. After watching the film with Chris Malloy and his brothers, the four of them dreamt of doing a similar trip of their own one day. Eventually the "forgotten film" would become the inspiration for Chris Malloy's film *180° South*. This is the original film canister for *Mountain of Storms*. The images that follow are frame grabs from that original film. Photo: Jeff Johnson

Somewhere on the Pan-American Highway. These were among the first 8-foot surfboards made – the shortboards of their time. Photo: Lito Tejada-Flores

After the asphalt turns to dirt: south of Mexico City along the Pan-American Highway. Mexico. Photos: Lito Tejada-Flores

Somewhere in Panama, without a Michelin Guide. Panama. Photo: Lito Tejada-Flores

Checking out the surf at Chicama, in northwest Peru. At 2.5 km it is one of the longest rideable breaks in the world. Chicama, Peru. Photo: Lito Tejada-Flores

Yvon Chouinard surfing the Chicama break. Chicama, Peru. Photo: Lito Tejada-Flores

Doug Tompkins at Chicama. Chicama, Peru. Photo: Lito Tejada-Flores

Stepping out of the van to get a first look at Fitz Roy. Cerro Fitz Roy, Patagonia. Photo: Lito Tejada-Flores

Riding the ferry for the lakes crossing from Puerto Montt, Chile, to Bariloche, Argentina. Argentine-Chilean border. Photo: Lito Tejada-Flores

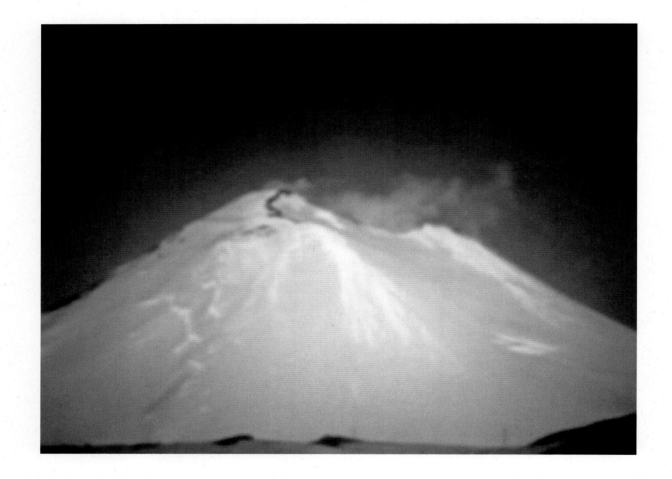

The fun hogs climbed the active volcano Mount Laima, then skied their way down. Chile. Photo: Lito Tejada-Flores

The fun hogs ascend Mount Osorno, Chile, shouldering skis for the trip down. Chile. Photo: Lito Tejada-Flores

On Fitz Roy. Patagonia. Photo: Lito Tejada-Flores

Yvon Chouinard on Cerro Fitz Roy, wearing the same Annapurna glasses (with leather side shields) he'd bring 40 years later to Corcovado and Cerro Kristine.
Cerro Fitz Roy, Patagonia. Photo: Lito Tejada-Flores

Hauling loads on the way to the base of Fitz Roy. Patagonia. Photo: Lito Tejada-Flores

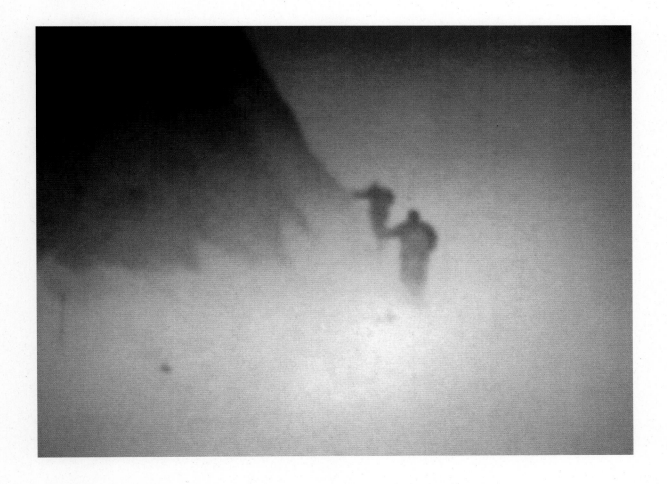

Near the base of Fitz Roy. Patagonia. Photo: Lito Tejada-Flores

Yvon Chouinard on the last difficult pitch, Fitz Roy. Patagonia. Photos: Lito Tejada-Flores

Near Fitz Roy's base. Patagonia. Photo: Lito Tejada-Flores

Chris Jones during the group's 31-day stay in the ice cave. Patagonia. Photo: Lito Tejada-Flores

Yvon Chouinard trying to keep a taut rope in high winds, outside the ice cave on Fitz Roy. Patagonia. Photo: Lito Tejada-Flores

Yvon Chouinard battling the wind, near the summit of Fitz Roy. Patagonia. Photo: Lito Tejada-Flores

Viva los Fun Hogs. At the summit of Fitz Roy. Patagonia. Photo: Lito Tejada-Flores

THE WAY TO 180° SOUTH

CHRIS MALLOY

When I saw the light, I realized the impact must have knocked me out. I was still 12 feet underwater and I had to put the pieces together fast. I was at Pipeline. I'd fallen on the vertical drop and got sucked back over the falls – twice. On the second revolution I'd bounced hard off the bottom.

I pulled toward the surface, following a shaft of light that lead through a clearing in the fizzing foam, praying I'd have time for at least one full breath before the next wave hit. I broke the surface and purged a mix of carbon dioxide, salt water, and vomit all in one massive exhale. Then I drew three deep breaths. Usually oxygen makes the spots go away, but not this time. The spots were closing in. My wave had been the first of the set and the horizon was black with at least four more bombs. I had 10 seconds before the first would detonate on the first reef, exactly where I was treading water.

Over the previous 10 years I had devoted my life to surfing Pipeline and had been in this situation before and survived. I knew there was no need to panic. Then I realized that I hadn't been in this exact situation; there was blood swirling in the foam around me and something big banging into my right leg. That something big turned out to be my left leg.

I had only seconds before the next wave broke. I had to make a choice: detach the leash from my dangling leg or keep it on. If I kept it on, as the wave broke the board would rip my left knee further out if its socket. If I let it go, I wouldn't have a board to float on, and I was still losing blood and already dizzy. And I had to make it through at least four quadruple overhead waves still stacked out to sea.

I kept the leash on, hoping to hold it tight enough to reduce the pull on my leg. The next wave hit, and the leash ripped from my hand as I cartwheeled in the whitewater. The leash stretched and my knee dislocated again; I had 10 seconds to the next wave. I had been hurt plenty of times before, but those injuries came out of nowhere and by the time I could realize what hit me, the danger had passed. This was different. This time I knew what was coming, and every wave was worse than the one before.

Old-timers say there are three stages to being a Pipe surfer: 1) I'll never get hurt; 2) there is a chance I could get hurt; 3) it's just a matter of time. Well, my time had come.

I finally drifted into the channel, snuck over the sandbar, and beached myself. Some friends who had seen what happened carried me to Jack Johnson's family lanai and put me in a chair under the big kamani tree. Jack's father walked over to hand me a towel and a cold beer. He had seen a hundred guys make or break their dreams at the Pipeline. He looked out to where Ka'ena Point meets the horizon, then asked, "So, what are you going to do now?"

For close to 15 years I had lived my dream. I left California for Hawai'i after high school to surf, freedive, and go to school. Through a combination of good luck and

Chris Malloy competing in the Eddie Aikau big-wave invitational contest in December of 2004. Waimea Bay, Oahu. Photo: Hank Foto

good timing, I had landed a modest sponsorship gig chasing storms and searching the globe for unridden spots. During my early twenties my friends and I were like migratory seabirds; we spent midwinter on the North Shore of Oahu, spring in Western Australia or South America, early summer in Tahiti, late summer in the Indonesian archipelago, then went back to Oahu. I also snuck in exploration trips to off-line spots in Papua New Guinea, the Philippines, New Caledonia, Samoa, Ireland, and even Antarctica.

On some of the islands I saw villages where no one but the elders had seen a white man, where people lived in ways I had been taught to call hand-to-mouth.

Each year I would return to the same villages and over a 12-year period witnessed great changes. It was like seeing a cultural time-lapse. On my first trip to Sumatra I remember a mother, her infant strapped to her back with palm fronds, going out every morning to the reef to throw her net. Each day the father took their older son out in a single-log canoe to fish the outer reef. In the evening this family would walk to a nearby village to trade some of their fish for rice and vegetables. I knew this life wasn't easy for them. It was hard work. But I could also see they looked healthy, and their kids looked happy.

Over the years I watched the family unravel. The father took a job on a tanker in Java and would be gone for months. The mother took a job cleaning bathrooms at a new hotel. Meanwhile a sales rep from a cigarette and soft drink company came through the village and like Johnny Appleseed, handed out free samples. The

family still lived in the same thatched hut, but the woman, cigarette hanging from her lips, now sat in a dark corner breastfeeding a new baby while the older kids swilled Coke. None of the family bothered any more to go fishing. A hundred generations of independence gone forever.

This image, and others like it, stuck with me. I got my hands on an old Canon and some black-and-white 35mm Ilford film and started to record the changes I saw. A few years later surf photographer Ted Grambeau, who had looked at some of my work, suggested we check out a photography exhibit in Aberdeen, Scotland, where we were traveling, to see the work of Sebastião Salgado and Henri Cartier-Bresson. I was amazed by their masterful composition and use of light, but moved by a deeper aspect of their work: Their images had captured the destruction of traditional life in the wake of the storm of modernity.

This was the theme I was after in my images, in part because of what I had seen in the villages, but also because of my background. I'd grown up in California, where my dad instilled a deep respect for farming and ranching in my brothers and me. I knew the condescension that the sophisticated assumed toward agrarian communities and people, and I also knew how vulnerable those people were in a consumer society based on corporate growth. I was also aware that I was becoming part of this corporate world, part of an exploding surf industry.

The morning after my accident at Pipeline, I peeled the bloody sheets from my knees and rolled on my side to get out of bed. My left leg, from the knee down,

A local couple. Maldive Islands. Photo: Chris Malloy

Chris Malloy with no chance for retreat at the Pipeline. North Shore, Oahu. Photos: Jeff Divine

Jack Johnson and Chris Malloy sift through a box of slide film. Santa Barbara, California. Photo: Grant Ellis

stayed exactly where it was, and my feet more or less faced opposite directions. At the hospital, the doctor pointed to the MRI and explained the damage: a badly torn meniscus, medial collateral, lateral collateral, and anterior cruciate ligaments all pretty much destroyed. He told me I needed reconstructive surgery, six months of rehab, and then I could walk again. I asked about surfing at the same level. "Not probable," he replied. As I crutched out of his office I recalled Jack's father the night before. "So what are you going to do now?"

Over the previous 10 years I had saved some money, and even before my wipeout had been thinking about making a surf film. I was disillusioned about how the surf industry had turned surfing into an "extreme" sport, and in turn how this influenced most surf films. Now I was looking at six long months out of the water and no security after that. It was either use the money to go back to school or dump it into a film. School didn't appeal, but there were a few problems with the film idea: I didn't know how to run a film camera. I didn't know the first thing about editing or editing machines. And I didn't know anything about the business side of filmmaking.

During a long and intense rehab program I started working to close my gaps as a filmmaker. My buddy Jack Johnson had just finished his film studies at the University of California-Santa Barbara, so I tracked him down in Europe where he was living in a van with his girlfriend. "Do you want to make a surf film?" I asked. He had no plans and no job. "Sure," he said. "I'll be home in a few weeks." I then called my cousin Emmett Malloy, who was working as a runner at a post-production house. I asked if he knew how to work an editing machine. "I'm getting the hang of it," he said. And if I wanted to make a film we could work at night when the editors were gone. "I also know where we could trade some telecine transfer time for a few surfboards," he added.

I filled four sketchpads with drawings and a notebook with ideas for music. My friends and I felt that our film should be about the past as well as the current moment. Rather than use these faraway places as aquatic gymnasiums for surf stunts, we wanted to share with a film audience how the cultures in those places helped shape the way we saw the modern world. We wanted to document good surfing, but the experience of place was even more important.

By the time Jack got home, my knee was starting to mend. We bought an old 16mm Bolex. Two weeks later we were out for our first footage, crossing a river in Burma, heading toward the Bay of Bengal and the Andaman Islands. Between travels I used an old typewriter to peck out letters to music labels, requesting rights to songs, while Emmett edited the film at night. We called it *Thicker than Water*, and its 1999 release barely earned mention in the surfing world. It didn't matter though, we had achieved our personal goal to make a film that reflected what we loved about surfing.

Then, slowly, friends began to pass the film to other friends. The surf shops started to order it. Little by little it gained momentum, enough that it looked as though we might be able to pay off our loan. Then, a year after release, the unimaginable happened: *Thicker than Water* won *Surfer Magazine*'s "Film of the Year" award.

I found myself back on Oahu with a film in the black and interested sponsors. I could now make more films, but I wanted to keep the scale small, to put together a little collective of filmmakers and musicians who were friends and family, including my brothers. We wanted to safeguard our independence and learn the process in our own way.

On Kona wind days my brothers and I would train at Waimea Bay, swimming, running in the sand, and bouldering on the volcanic rock on the west side. One day we found North Shore lifeguard Jeff Johnson on the same program. He gave us some climbing tips and soon we were spending more time bouldering than running or swimming.

When a house on the beach became available, and we needed another roommate to make the rent, Jeff seemed like the perfect fit. Before long we were calling him "the fourth brother." Jeff and I had a lot in common. We had both grown up in small inland towns in California – he was from Danville and I was from Ojai – and had both moved to the North Shore in our teens. We shared a deep appreciation for the history of surfing, and – new for me – a love for climbing. We both had archives of out-of-print films and books, and after a day in the water, liked nothing better than to crack a cold beer and nerd out on what it would have been like to run with Pat Curren, Buzzy Trent, Chuck Pratt, Yvon Chouinard, or Edward Abbey.

My brothers and I had lucked into the free ride of pro surfing, but Jeff had come up on his own. He left school at 16, started sneaking into abandoned houses to skateboard empty swimming pools, and worked construction to pay for his boards. On Oahu he had become a member of the highly respected crew of watermen that make up the North Shore lifeguards.

He also worked as a flight attendant so he could travel the world, and for the past five years had pinballed between climbing and surfing trips almost nonstop, all on his own dime.

One evening Jeff and I, poring over an old climbing book, came across an account of the first ascent of Yosemite's Half Dome. When we saw the date – 1957 – we looked at each other in disbelief. The first big wall to be climbed and the first big wave to be ridden were both in the same year. A small team of ragtag climbers, led by Royal Robbins, in June made the first ascent of Half Dome's vertical northwest face, a feat then thought impossible. In November, a crew of surfers led by Greg Noll and Pat Curren paddled into Waimea Bay. We had been nurturing this idea that climbing and surfing had a lot in common, and here it was right in front of us: surfing and climbing, twins separated at birth.

I began to read more about the history of both sports and also about the context in which they evolved. By the late '50s America had gone from the "land of the free" to the land of the "nine-to-five" – with nothing seen as worthwhile unless it turned a profit or provided security. Unaware of each other, two different groups split off from the mass culture to travel parallel paths. They traded middle-class prosperity and security for adventure, self-reliance, and a connection to the natural world. The two tribes, largely unknown to each other, lived similar lives. They were all dead broke, building and inventing their own gear as they went along.

Ten years later, in Ventura, California, two epic dirtbags crossed paths. Yvon Chouinard, one of America's best climbers, and Bob McTavish, one of Australia's best surfers, ended up working a few yards away from each other. They lived hand-to-mouth on the same beach, building equipment that would change forever their respective disciplines. Yvon

An appreciation for history led Chris Malloy on trips to seek out people like Miki Dora, Bob McTavish, John Kelly, and Pat Curren.
Here, Chris has a chance encounter with North Shore pioneer Pat Curren. Baja, Mexico. Photo: Tom Servais

Late 1950s big-wave pioneers at Waimea Bay. O'ahu, Hawai'i. Photo: Don James

Early big-wall pioneers Royal Robbins, Tom Frost, and Yvon Chouinard on the first ascent of the North America Wall, El Capitan. Yosemite, California. Photo: Chuck Pratt

Inspired by the film *Mountain of Storms*, Chris Malloy and Jeff Johnson set out for Australia to film a climbing and surfing road trip of their own.
While their filming effort dwindled, the trip would prove to be a precursor to Chris's film *180° South* nearly a decade later. The Watchtower Crack, Mount Arapiles, Australia. Photo: Scott Soens

in his tin shed forged the first hard-steel pitons suitable for multiple placements on big granite walls. McTavish in his Quonset hut was chopping feet off old-style longboards to help usher in the shortboard revolution.

Years later when I asked each of them what his prime motivation was during that time, they gave precisely the same answer: "I was after the cleanest line on the steepest part of the face."

For Jeff and me, the kindred spirit of being in the ocean and being in the mountains played out in long surf sessions in the morning at places like Sunset and Phantoms, followed by even longer climbing sessions in the afternoons at newly discovered crags near Ka'ena Point. The wheels began to turn in my head. A film with climbing and surfing might be possible, one whose images and music inspired people with a sense of place.

One evening, after returning from a trip to Joshua Tree and Yosemite, Jeff cracked open a couple of beers and handed me a beat-up VHS tape with "FITZ ROY" scribbled on the spine. "You gotta' check this out," he said. "It's gonna blow your mind."

The story that unfolded in *Mountain of Storms* did blow my mind. The year was 1968, and Yvon Chouinard and Doug Tompkins, with their friends Lito Tejada-Flores and Dick Dorworth, loaded climbing gear and surfboards into an old Ford Econoline van for a six-month journey to Patagonia, surfing and climbing along the way. And at the end they put up a new route on Fitz Roy, the iconic peak of the region. Lito's wind-up 16mm Bolex captured the essence of what I felt to be the common spirit between climbing and surfing – the spirit of these pioneers finding their own way in an increasingly complicated world.

I had read about Conservación Patagónica, Doug and Kristine Tompkins' effort to save and restore millions of acres of wilderness in southern Argentina and Chile, and I knew that Yvon Chouinard was involved as well. I also knew that Yvon donated 1 percent of Patagonia's sales to wildlands conservation. Something started to click for me: that *Mountain of Storms* had documented something larger than an adventure; the experience may have played a big role in setting these two guys on their paths as environmental philanthropists.

Shortly after Jeff showed me the film, he and I crammed as much climbing gear as possible into our board bags and took off for Melbourne. Scott Soens, director of photography for my film *Shelter*, came along to shoot. Jeff had made a few calls to score gear and lucked into Patagonia's testing program, which got us free clothes in exchange for feedback on the product. We were operating on a smaller budget than usual and the first priority of the trip was to have as much fun as possible. We surfed the reefs of Victoria and climbed the crags of Mount Arapiles, and each night I crawled into my sleeping bag totally exhausted. One of Jeff's journal entries tells it best:

My hands have woken me up. They feel as if they've been slammed in a car door. They're swollen, riddled with scabs, and my fingertips are raw. I shake them out above my head and lie there in my sleeping bag. I can hear Scott and Chris sleeping. "Okay," I say to myself. "I'm in a room, but what room? Where?"

The sky begins to glow behind ratty old curtains. I get out of bed and walk to the kitchen of the 150-year-old farmhouse to boil water for coffee. Standing on the back porch watching the stars go dim, I expect my well-trained ears to hear the ocean, my sensitive nose to smell salt. But there is nothing, only silence and dust. A few minutes later, Scott and Chris stammer in dragging duffel bags and backpacks. I slide a cup to Chris and offer one to Scott. Scott smiles, rubbing sleep from his eyes, and asks our daily question: "Where are we going?"

"I don't know," says Chris as he inspects the scabs on his hands from yesterday's climb. "But I'd love to get these things into some salt water."

It seems like we're in the middle of nowhere, land-locked in Natimuk, a small, dusty town straight out of a spaghetti western: one road, one bar, one general store. After 20-some-odd days of being on the road, the three of us have grown accustomed to perpetual movement. Last night we received a report from the coast saying a swell is on the way and the winds are good. Our car is now stuffed to the ceiling, our board bags strapped to the roof, and the stereo is loud. Mount Arapiles fades on the horizon, Scott is at the wheel, and Chris and I sip our coffee watching the countryside streak by. We have only two days left and we need waves.

Thirty days later we returned home with scabbed hands, sunburned faces, and a new understanding of what Patagonia's "Ironclad Guarantee" was all about. I was increasingly curious about Yvon Chouinard, how he had started as a penniless climber, surfer, and craftsman, and ended with a multimillion-dollar corporation. I had read of his animosity toward big business, yet here he was running one, albeit one that sounded a little quirky. I'd be coming through California in late summer, and I planned to spend a few days tracking him down.

I finally met Yvon in the water. He sat out the back at a small point break, quietly waiting for sets. For an hour I just watched him surf, and there was something about

him that reminded me less of a businessman, or even an environmentalist, and more of my dad and uncles, who were pipeliners and cowboys. Finally, I worked up the gumption to introduce myself. He was surprised that I'd gotten my hands on the obscure *Mountain of Storms*. He told me about some of his favorite fly-fishing spots and turned me on to a recipe for buffalo meat. When a set swung his way, however, he didn't hesitate to break off. When he paddled back out I told him that Jeff Johnson and I wanted to someday follow a route like his to Patagonia. He sat up on his board, looked out to sea and said, "Well, you'd better go now. The bastards are damming the place to hell and poisoning all the river mouths with pulp mills."

In the coming months my brothers and I started surfing and climbing with Yvon. One morning he took us into the Sespe, a climbing wall he had pioneered in the 1960s. We couldn't help but notice his climbing gear was archaic. He handed us an old swami belt, and then started up the rock while we had to figure out on our own out how to belay him. Later we had dinner at his house and I started browsing his bookshelf. He showed me passages from Wendell Berry and Aldo Leopold, and we talked late into the evening about how they and others had influenced his philosophy as well as his approach to business. Still, I was skeptical. I just assumed, a little cynically, that the more I got to know Yvon, and especially the more I learned about his company, the more I'd see they were like all the rest.

But then I ran across one of his old catalogs with an essay he had written titled "Don't Buy This Jacket." The article encouraged Patagonia's customers to not buy a new jacket until they had worn out their old one. That got the wheels turning. There was nothing in that position you could label as marketing bullshit, and I concluded that Yvon's mantra to "use business

Chris Malloy with gaucho Erasmo Betancore during the filming of *180° South*. Valle Chacabuco, Chile. Photo: Scott Soens

Director Chris Malloy on location. Patagonia, Chile. Photo: Scott Soens

to make change" was legit. At the end of summer I hit the road with a backpack full of books from his shelf. I wouldn't see him for another year, but my brothers and I used his clothes on some cold-weather travel to the Orkney Islands and Canada in search of unridden surf. Our respect for him grew.

The following summer, my brothers and I returned home to find out that our sponsor of close to 15 years had gone public and was on the verge of a big expansion into the fashion market. They had treated us like family, supporting our surfing and filmmaking through thick and thin, but I didn't want to go where they wanted to go. I told Jeff in confidence that my brothers and I were seriously considering walking away from the surf industry.

We started surfing and hanging with Yvon again. He was guarded now and so were we, but eventually we began to circle around the "what if" of us working with him to bring his methods of business to a whole new world: the surf industry. There were already some pieces to work with. Yvon's son Fletcher was a good shaper, and he had been working on a new and smarter way of building longer-lasting boards. Yvon had been building good board shorts for over a decade, but they both had gone largely unnoticed because they weren't part of the "scene."

Jeff could see the writing on the wall and, unbeknownst to my brothers and me, had talked with Yvon about the possibility of a partnership. Yvon saw the value in working with us, but there were gaps to close. He didn't want to pay us just to ride and get cover shots. The few athletes he paid were expected to really work for the company. On our end, we knew we would make far less than we had been making.

Finally my brothers and I reached the point where we had to follow the gut more than the head. We called our sponsor and asked to be let out of our four-year contract. They graciously let us go, and a week later we shook hands with Yvon and Fletcher, and together we became partners in a new mission: bring Patagonia's revolutionary business ideas to the surfing community.

That first year we spent every day we were in town in the office, working on clothing designs and catalogs. If Patagonia was going to build a new surf line, we were going to be involved in it, beginning to end. But we were also expected to continue to live the kinds of lives that had made us a good fit in the first place. And for me, that meant continuing to look for surf, and to think about making another film.

Rick Ridgeway and I talked over what that next film might be. Rick, one of Yvon's best friends, headed up Patagonia's marketing department and its environmental initiatives program. He was a surfer and climber – and a writer and filmmaker – who was also deeply involved with Doug and Kris Tompkins and Yvon in Conservación Patagónica.

Rick listened as I told him how inspired I'd been by *Mountain of Storms*, that I wanted to film a road trip that combined climbing and surfing – and before long we brainstormed an idea that excited us both. Why not a modern-day remake of the 1968 trip? Exactly 40 years later, we could get a team together to leave from Ventura on a surfing and climbing trip all the way to Patagonia.

Rick then pulled out a map and showed me a section of the Patagonian coastline where Conservación

Patagónica had recently created a new national park. Here was a mountain he and Yvon had talked about climbing. It looked like the Matterhorn only it rose right above the beach, on one of the most amazing coastlines he'd ever seen.

I thought about it. The mountain sounded good, but what about the surf? I knew that once you got far enough south on the Chilean coastline, there was an unbroken chain of islands offshore that blocked any waves from hitting the mainland. "Yes," Rick said, pointing to the map, "except maybe right here, where the mountain is. See this breach in the offshore islands? If a swell hit from just the right angle, it would also hit the coast."

A month later Rick and I were in a small plane crossing a fjord on our way to visit Parque Pumalín, one of the projects created by Conservación Patagónica. For a decade I'd dreamt of seeing this place. The fact that Yvon was there too, working with Doug and Kris, made it that much more special. My first view of the Reñihué fjord, where Doug and Kris had their home, and where the park had its administrative center, was staggering: a deep fjord framed by steep walls covered with beech forests, and in the back a huge glacier-covered volcano.

We rendezvoused at Doug and Kris's house, and around the dinner table I started to learn about the 15-year struggle to create Parque Pumalín in the face of Chilean suspicions of a rich American buying so much property that it literally cut the country in half. I also learned about Doug and Kris's commitment to using sustainable farming and ranching practices. I had seen firsthand in North America the bitter struggles over land use between the "leave it alone" camp and the "manifest destiny" camp. But here was a new vision, a new idea of how to effect land conservation.

By our second day at Pumalín, we had maps spread out on the table. Rick pointed to the Corcovado peak that was the centerpiece of the new Corcovado National Park, another project created by the Tompkinses' land trust. Rick pointed to the small breach in the otherwise continuous chain of barrier islands and repeated his idea about the possibility of a swell sneaking through and hitting the mainland. If Rick's theory proved true, it would be a perfect setup: waves that have never been ridden directly in front of a stunning mountain that had only been climbed once, and that was by Doug. I was still skeptical.

We took off in Doug's small Cessna and for the next hour, flew over high alpine valleys framed by feathering waterfalls, then over the volcano covered in a dozen square miles of brilliant-white glaciers. And it was all part of the largest privately owned park in the world. We crossed a bay and ahead in the distance loomed the stunning tower of Corcovado peak. As we neared the coast I looked at the shoreline and… it was flat. There was no whitewater at all.

From the backseat I heard Rick yell, "We're not there yet." There was a prominent point coming up and as we rounded it, I saw the slightest indication of waves. We rounded another point, and the waves increased. After another 10 miles I was looking out the window at a near-perfect right, maybe four to five feet high, crossing a bay that had never seen a surfboard. I couldn't believe my eyes. We circled back and flew over the spot again. On land, a beautiful waterfall dropped from a short cliff onto a cobblestone beach. In the water another

Chilean gaucho near Pichilemu, Chile. Photographed and framed by Chris Malloy for his cousin Emmett Malloy. Photo: Chris Malloy

set arrived, and I watched it peel right cross the bay. I turned around and yelled back to Rick, "We got ourselves a movie!"

In the months to come, Rick and I pondered the team we might put together to retrace a route inspired by the 1968 trip. We both realized that if the film was to succeed, it would need to not only capture the dynamic elements of surfing and climbing, but also explore how that original trip had been such a catalyst in setting Yvon and Doug on their paths as wildlands philanthropists and adventurers. What was it about Patagonia, the place, that had made such an impact on their lives?

To put our team together we had access to the most famous climbers and surfers in the world. But that route didn't seem right to me. Whoever followed in Yvon and Doug's footsteps had to be someone who, like them, had dedicated his life to experiencing the world. One evening, as Jeff and I were mulling over the list, I realized that no one was even remotely as qualified as he. He was intelligent, self-educated, and independent – and a gifted photographer and writer. Jeff was the one who'd found the old footage, and it was also his real dream to retrace their journey. I didn't care that he wasn't a big name, or a name at all. He was the person for this trip. I called Rick and we made our decision that night.

I asked Jeff to pick the best climber and the best surfer that he knew to go along. He chose Timmy O'Neill as

the climber and my brother Keith as surfer. These guys were pros, but they were real friends of Jeff's, and they were guys who had put in some hard miles together.

The next question was how to get there. Rick had a solid background in sailing and raised the idea of jumping on a boat and heading south. We loved the idea, but chartering a boat felt wrong for the spirit of the trip, not to mention the budget. Not giving up, Rick connected with the sailing community and put the word out. Soon he got word that a young guy was readying a boat in Seattle to head south to the Chilean coast. It was a one-in-a-million chance. We had little time to prep, and Jeff actually missed the boat when it came through Ventura. We had only one more shot: if Jeff could drive four days straight, from Ventura to Ixtapa, where the boat was stopping for re-supply, he could join in on the five-month sail, then surf the Chilean coastline and climb Corcovado with his heroes Yvon and Doug.

Jeff made the boat. The rest is his story, as seen through his camera and recorded in his notebooks. And Yvon and Doug's story too, as told around the fire.

THE JOURNEY

JEFF JOHNSON

MOUNTAIN OF STORMS

1. In 1968, Yvon Chouinard, Doug Tompkins, Dick Dorworth, and Lito Tejada-Flores pack up their 1965 Ford Econoline van in Ventura, California, and begin the long drive south to climb Cerro Fitz Roy in Patagonia, Chile.

2. Sleeping on the ground in Guatemala, they wake up to teenagers holding guns to their heads.

3. Dick Dorworth cuts Yvon's hair as the four travelers kill time in the port town of Colón, Panama, as they wait for a boat to take them into Colombia.

4. Yvon Chouinard breaks his neck jumping off a bridge in Colombia.

5. Doug Tompkins and Yvon Chouinard get the best waves of their trip surfing Chicama in northern Peru.

6. The van breaks down in the city of Santiago, Chile. They pull the engine and rebuild it on the spot.

7. The four of them climb and ski an active volcano called Mount Llaima, southeast of Santiago, Chile.

8. North of Cerro Fitz Roy, in the Patagonia desert, they pick up English climber Chris Jones hitchhiking by the side of the road.

9. Yvon Chouinard, Doug Tompkins, Dick Dorworth, Chris Jones, and Lito Tejada-Flores summit Cerro Fitz Roy via a new route they name Ruta de los Californianos.

180° SOUTH

A. Keith Malloy and Jeff Johnson join up with Timmy O'Neill and Dave Turner to climb the North America Wall in Yosemite, California.

B. In Ixtapa, Mexico, Jeff Johnson boards a 54-foot cutter-rigged sailboat called the *Seabear* bound for Patagonia, Chile.

C. Roughly 300 miles southwest of the Osa Peninsula, Costa Rica, the *Seabear* and crew have a four-day stopover at Isla de Coco National Park.

D. After a tough nine-day crossing the *Seabear* and crew enter the Galápagos Archipelago, Ecuador.

E. Nine days into the passage to Rapa Nui (Easter Island) the *Seabear* loses her mast 400 miles short of her destination.

F. The *Seabear* and crew anchor off Rapa Nui for 36 days to repair their mast. While there, they befriend local surfer Makohe Acuna and invite her to join them on the sail to Chile.

G. En route to Chile, with jury-rigged mast and sails, the *Seabear* and crew spend two days on Isla de Juan Fernandez, 400 miles off the coast of mainland Chile.

H. The *Seabear* and crew arrive at Algarrobo, Chile. Makohe Acuna and Jeff Johnson part ways with the *Seabear* and meet up with Keith Malloy farther south.

I. Makohe Acuna, Keith Malloy, and Jeff Johnson rendezvous with Timmy O'Neill and Yvon Chouinard in Reñihué, Chile.

J. Makohe Acuna, Keith Malloy, Jeff Johnson, Timmy O'Neill, and Yvon Chouinard explore the Corcovado coast of Chile aboard a retired fishing boat called the *Cahuelmo*.

K. Doug Tompkins, Yvon Chouinard, and Jeff Johnson climb Cerro Geezer in Valle Chacabuco, Chile.

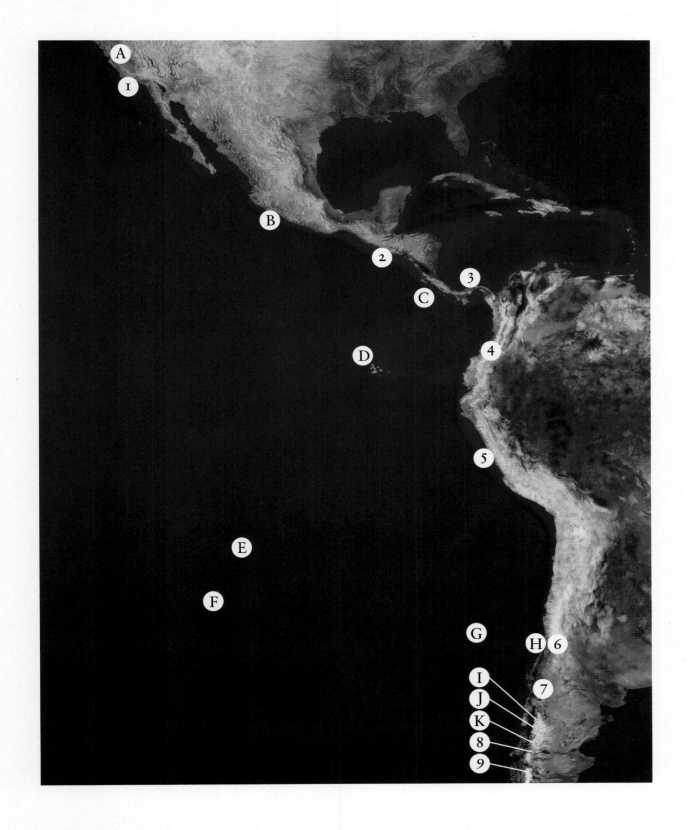

YOSEMITE VALLEY

Keith is 20 feet off the ground hanging in a ponderosa pine, the massive granite walls of Yosemite Valley towering around. He spins in circles, tangled in a mess of webbing and rope.

Timmy yells to him, trying to explain things. "When you extend your right ascender your daisy chain should be within an arm's reach, your feet should be even in your étriers."

Keith stares at the rat's nest of gear in front of him. He says nothing.

"Keith," Timmy says. "You know what I mean?"

"Um… no, not really."

"Okay," Timmy continues, "if you're sketched out, weight your upper ascender and put on your Grigri. Suck your weight onto the Grigri, take off your ascender, and rappel. Back yourself up with a chicken knot if that makes you feel better."

There is a long pause. "What?" says Keith.

Timmy looks at the ground. "We need another guy to go with us," he says desperately. He eyes a few friends who have been checking our progress. "I'm going to need some help up there."

Keith is silent, trying to come to terms with this confusion in a tree and how it applies to climbing the 3,000-foot wall of El Capitan. He bites his lower lip and chews his beard – a habit that will grow increasingly worse over the next week.

The next morning Keith and I wait for Timmy in the El Cap meadow. We kneel over our random assortment of gear spread out on a blue tarp. It's calm, quiet – a few climbers huddle together, drink coffee, and watch the sun light up the southeast wall of the Captain.

Timmy pulls up in his car around 9 o'clock. His stereo blasts an early 1980s cheese-ball song. He sings at the top of his lungs and dances seductively like an androgynous glam rocker, rubbing himself all over, swaying and winking to an imaginary crowd.

Timmy is hung-over again. Drunk even. His thick, reddish-brown hair is matted on one side of his head and pokes out like small cathedrals on the other, his eyes red as embers. While Keith and I have been rushing around the Valley trying to get our shit squared away for the climb, Timmy has enjoyed what he declares to be the biggest party week he's seen in Yosemite.

Like a small whirlwind he dances toward us. "Oh my God," he says. "Are you two monks? You guys missed it again. More chicks than ever last night – dirty dancing! Pelvises like Elvis's grinding all over the place."

Wound tight like a golf ball's rubber-band innards, Timmy rolls up his sleeves, exposing his veiny forearms, and dumps out the contents of a haul bag. He introduces us to Dave Turner, the guy he has recruited to join us on the North America Wall. Dave is tall and lanky, quiet and casual. He's known for rope-soloing the hardest aid lines on El Capitan.

Previous spread: Yosemite Valley as seen from Tunnel View. The west face of El Capitan on the left, Bridalveil Falls on the right, Half Dome in the far distance. Yosemite, California. Photo: Jeff Johnson

Timmy O'Neill racking up for the North America Wall. El Capitan Meadow, Yosemite, California. Photo: Jeff Johnson

Keith Malloy and Timmy O'Neill bivouac in the infamous Black Cave on the North America Wall. El Capitan, Yosemite, California. Photo: Jeff Johnson

Keith has grown quieter as the days count down. He fumbles through a bunch of carabiners, fiddles with a wall-hauler, and throws it onto the heap. He stares up at El Capitan, one of the world's tallest granite walls, one that he'll be climbing in less than a day, a wall he called Half Dome while talking to someone on the phone last night.

The next morning we wake up on Mazatlán ledge. Thousands of feet of granite tower over us, nothing below but air. Timmy and Dave share their first 50/50 "cigarette" of the day. Keith remains deep in his sleeping bag, pressed between the wall and Timmy. He doesn't move, he doesn't say a word.

In the fall of 1964, Royal Robbins, Tom Frost, Chuck Pratt, and Yvon Chouinard – the dream team of their era – assembled to attempt the unclimbed North America Wall on the southeast face of El Capitan. After 10 days of climbing, battling rain and snow, they topped out on what was considered at the time the hardest rock climb in the world. Things are different now. The gear has improved and many have climbed this route since, but there remains an unbelievable amount of stress involved – both physical and mental.

Our crew is definitely not a "dream team." Timmy is a speed freak – a fast-moving, impatient, top-notch climber. Dave is extraordinarily mellow – has everything so dialed he could do this in his sleep. Keith is mere luggage – an accomplished big-wave surfer, but not a climber by any standards. And I have done just enough of these climbs to be dangerous.

Later, at a belay, Timmy lights his fourth 50/50 of the morning and says, "Oh my God. I can't believe we're doing this. I've been up El Cap something like twenty-five times and it still freaks me out. I mean look where we are. It's crazy. You'd think I'd get used to it, but no."

He blows out a plume of smoke, pauses in thought, then yells, "Okay, Meaty Malloy! Put your jugs on that thing and haul!" Keith and I have become haul monkeys, counterweights as we drag an absurd amount of gear up the face. Dave is on lead, quietly gaining distance above.

It is morning again and we're hanging in a bottomless alcove 1,600 feet off the ground. Everyone else is asleep. Light seeps over the horizon and drips like hot oil down the cold wall of the cave. I peek out over the portaledge, straight down to the valley floor. It's strange to feel enclosed and protected but still very exposed.

Timmy wakes up. I hear him say, "No. We're still here? Damn it. I thought I was dreaming."

Morning moves slowly. We're all tired, but Keith still hasn't said much and I'm beginning to worry. "Keith," I say. "Keith…" A long pause, and then he mumbles something from inside his sleeping bag.

The next day I wake to a light tapping sound on our rain fly. I stick my camera out the bottom of the fly and take a shot. I pull it back in; the entire LCD screen is white. We are floating in a cloud high above the earth. I listen to the snowflakes dancing on the fly, a lullaby rhythm increasing and decreasing with each gust of wind. Mesmerized, I fall back to sleep.

All day and night we are trapped in the Cyclops Eye, a 200-foot-high and 30-foot-deep indentation three-quarters of the way up the wall. In the calm between storm flurries, we crawl from our bivies and congregate on the narrow ledges. We share food, pass beers around, and drink French-pressed coffee. Timmy and Dave roll one cigarette after another. Dave takes out his solar-powered iPod and dances precariously on a tiny ledge. Next to him Keith, curled up in his sleeping bag, clutches at whatever he can get his hands on.

Farthest to the right is local legend Sean "Stanley" Leary. He was attempting to free climb El Niño, a variation of the original North America route, with his partner, who is hidden within the yellow portaledge. The storm forced the two teams to congregate in the Cyclops Eye for two nights until it cleared. North America Wall, El Capitan, Yosemite, California. Photo: Jeff Johnson

Timmy O'Neill, Sean Leary, and Dave Turner wait out the storm in the Cyclops Eye. The North America Wall on El Capitan, Yosemite, California. Photo: Jeff Johnson

Dark clouds pour in over the walls of Yosemite Valley and fill the valley floor. Then, with a light updraft, the clouds creep slowly up the wall and engulf us. Snowflakes appear in the whiteout, whipping around our faces. We crawl back into our cocoons and wait. The last thing I remember before drifting off to sleep is Johnny Cash's voice piercing the dull silence of snow, "I hurt myself today, to see if I still feel. I focus on the pain, the only thing that's real."

We wake the next morning to bluebird conditions. It is cold, crisp, and unbelievably clear. The storm has set us back two days, and we've begun to ration food and water. Keith is showing rare signs of excitement.

In our first real conversation in five days, Keith says, "I don't like sitting around. I like having something to do. It keeps my mind off the height."

We lower him out over the abyss, 2,000 feet of air below and nothing but sky above. He yelps – a muffled attempt to yodel, but with his heart in his throat. I think of a Royal Robbins quote during an interview in his later years. He said, "You climb because you are afraid."

We top out in the afternoon of the seventh day and head for the east ledges. The descent is the sketchiest part of the whole climb, almost worse than the climb itself. At least on the climb you are protected by the anchors you place. Here we have nothing but huge, awkward haul bags strapped to our backs. We're tired, we're anxious – one slip on the steep slabs could result in a hundred cartwheels followed by a 2,000-foot free-fall.

I remember how the first time I climbed El Capitan, I vowed, while on this same descent, to never do it again. And here I am again, the third time, stumbling down a trail, cursing my selective memory. I keep an eye on Keith. I can tell he is definitely not going to do this again.

Back at Curry Village I sleep heavily in my van while Keith finds a bed in one of the canvas tents. I get up early the next day and go for a walk, thinking Keith would sleep in. Surprised, I find him standing near the pizza deck, a huge smile on his face, drinking a large coffee.

"Whoa," I say. "Why are you up so early?"

"Man," he replies, "I couldn't sleep. I was so excited to just walk around, see new faces, not have to worry about dying all the time."

Keith pulls out his wallet and holds it out in front of his face. "Watch this!" he says, and drops the wallet on the floor. "See, just pick it up. Ha! No problem! Ha, ha!"

There is a long pause as he studies the flow of ambling tourists. "Hey," he says looking straight into my eyes, a wide smile, his ice-blue eyes glowing. "That was the toughest seven days of my entire life."

Keith Malloy jugs above the Cyclops Eye. The North America Wall on El Capitan, Yosemite, California. Photo: Jeff Johnson

Timmy O'Neill and Keith Malloy waking up in the Igloo, two pitches from the summit, last day on
the North America Wall. El Capitan, Yosemite, California. Photo: Jeff Johnson

Keith Malloy and Dave Turner in the Igloo, two pitches from the summit of the North America Wall. El Capitan, Yosemite, California. Photo: Jeff Johnson

DRIVING SOUTH

I woke up somewhere outside of Indio, eastbound on the I-10. It was hot, my eyes were dry, and my muscles cramped from beating myself up on El Capitan then jumping into a car and sitting. A friend of a friend told me that this guy Mike would be driving down to Zihuatanejo in early October. If I pitched in for gas he could give me a ride.

So there we were – two strangers in a Chevy Suburban with a pit bull-Labrador mix named Indy – driving south in the ever-increasing heat. So far I had just been sleeping. Mike had been silent, listening to music, patiently watching the road. When I woke up, I said hello and he nodded and smiled. I drifted back to sleep.

The slowing of the engine awakened me again. It was midnight and we were stopped on the side of a dark road near the town of Navajoa. Mike was talking with a federale outside. I know very little Spanish, but from the sound of the conversation and friendly gestures I figured he was helping us, maybe giving us directions. Mike came back to the cab with a sharp gleam in his eye. "He's taking us for three hundred dollars," he said. "Some bullshit about my registration. Three hundred dollars or he impounds the car and everything in it."

In the rearview mirror I watched Mike count bills into the federale's open hand while his other hand held back the tail of his jacket exposing a holstered revolver. The federale looked casual, a slight grin on his face. Mike returned to the cab angry, almost laughing. "He says he'll escort us out of here so we don't get pulled over again."

We followed the brand-new, government issued, four-wheel-drive SUV toward the highway. By the side of the road we saw two more cars that had been pulled over by federales. Surprisingly they were Mexican families, not tourists – luggage and furniture tied to the roofs of their cars, sullen faces counting bills into open hands.

Mike drove as far as his eyes would allow, and at around 2 am we pulled into a no-tell hotel near Los Mochis. Every town along this road seemed to have a by-the-hour place where men take their mistresses, or vice versa. Mike pulled off the highway and a man pulled a gate open for us. We followed him, idling past rows of blue tarps that hung over parking stalls and hid the parked cars, keeping identities a secret.

The room was dirty and odd looking. A sad attempt at a Byzantine motif: cracked cement columns, arched doorways, a cement floor with thin, coarse carpet. Pillows made of cardboard. Mike took the bed; I slept on the floor with Indy. In the morning we found condom wrappers in the bathroom and an empty packet of Viagra. I made coffee on a lopsided lamp shelf below a light that burned out as soon as I turned it on. We left just after sunrise.

Previous spread: Keith Malloy and Jeff Johnson part ways after the climb, and Jeff ventures south to catch a boat in Mexico that is headed for Patagonia, Chile. Photo: Jeff Johnson

Coconut farmer and his daughter. Tecomán, Mexico. Photo: Jeff Johnson

Local surfers spar on the beach. Near Manzanillo, Mexico. Photos: Jeff Johnson

Isla de Janitzio, Lago de Pátzcuaro, Mexico. Photo: Jeff Johnson

Some believe the island villagers are the purest of the P'urhépecha bloodline. Only the young villagers speak Spanish while the old, some of whom have never left the island, hold on to their language and traditional ways. Isla de Janitzio, Lago de Pátzcuaro, Mexico. Photo: Jeff Johnson

LEAVING SIGHT OF LAND

I have surfaced from one of the worst hangovers of my life: a two-day delirium resulting from a bon voyage party in Ixtapa. I am aboard the *Seabear* approaching the Gulf of Tehuantepec. I can barely remember getting our passports stamped in Acapulco.

Those who have never crossed a large expanse of ocean in a small boat have no idea what's involved. When I mentioned this trip to friends and acquaintances before leaving – how I planned to sail with strangers to Chile – their response was always the same.

"Oh," they'd say, their face suddenly glowing. "I wish I could go." Their eyes glazed over as they drifted off to an imaginary place: clear blue water, sunny skies, the anchor set in a beautiful bay. They imagine themselves tanned, swirling a straw around in some exotic fruit drink. And there's the sailing part: them perched at the bow, wind blowing through their hair – bleached now by countless days in the sun – approaching a mysterious island just on the horizon.

I know about this. I had similar visions before I agreed to help a guy get his boat from Hawai'i to Tahiti. I had never really sailed before and a crossing sounded so romantic. I brought my guitar, my journal, and my yoga mat. I had never done yoga before, but I thought this would be a great time to start. For 20-some-odd days, I was barely able to use any of these things. The crossing was too rough, our world turned – almost literally – upside down.

Crossings are like jail time, only prettier. They alternate between extremely boring and absolutely terrifying. In some ways they are worse than jail: fewer people to talk to, less space to move around in, and your world is in constant movement, 24/7. It never stops: not while you pee, brush your teeth, eat lunch, fix dinner, or shuffle from one small area of the boat to another. Bouncing, rolling, lurching, slamming, rocking – it never stops. You can only tell or listen to so many stories, read so many books, watch so many videos, listen to so many songs. Eventually you just sit there and stare at the same things you've been staring at for how many days you care not to remember. But you do know, down to the hour, when you think you will hit land. And all you can think about is that day: the day you get out.

Then again, there are those moments, the reasons I subject myself to such abuse. The nights alone at the helm, sitting under the stars, thinking about life, the world, the universe. Or, after having endured the crossing, you set foot on foreign land and have earned it, much more than if you had taken a commercial flight to get there. You see things you never would have seen had you not sailed there. But these are moments, mind you. And this is only one opinion coming from a person who loves the ocean, has spent a great amount of time in the ocean, but who gets queasy at the very mention of a crossing.

Such are my thoughts as we lose sight of land, watching Mexico's Sierra Madre fade in the far distance, crossing the Gulf of Tehuantepec, angling out over open ocean toward Islas del Coco off Costa Rica. We batten down the hatches and prepare for what could be some of the roughest waters of the entire journey. My queasy stomach rises to my throat as we reef in the mainsail. I'm thinking about that Hawai'i-to-Tahiti crossing, one of the greatest experiences of my entire life, and how in Papeete over cold Hinano beers I vowed never to do that again. Never. And shit, look at me now: once again the victim of selective memory. What an imbecile.

Dave McGuire checks the rigging aboard the *Seabear*. Halfway between Isla de Coco and the Galápagos Islands. Photo: Jeff Johnson

Trolling for fish with a hand line off the back of the *Seabear*. Off the coast of Mexico. Photo: Jeff Johnson

The *Seabear* anchored among diving and fishing boats in Chatham Bay. Isla de Coco, Costa Rica. Photo: Jeff Johnson

IT'S NOT AN ADVENTURE

I took the helm for the 6 am watch. During the watch change, Allen Szydlowski told me that he and Timmy had reefed the mainsail and reduced the headsail; strong winds gusted to more than 30 knots. The boat speed was our fastest yet. Though the gusts had dropped a bit, he said to take heed. If we got overpowered again, I was to wake him up, and we'd take in more headsail.

I stepped out of the cockpit to take a piss and looked forward: The entire starboard rail was awash. It was nothing unusual, just good sailing. But I noticed the boat speed had dropped some, the wind had backed off, and the headsail was luffing – the rigging clanging against the mast. The wind angle had moved forward, so I altered the course a few clicks to starboard – west – to fill the sails once again. At 8 am everything looked good.

I went below deck to make myself a bowl of cereal. Half an hour later, I was sitting at the helm again, eating my cereal and looking out the front window of the enclosed cockpit. Aside from tiny patches of sky, all I could see were the mast and the headsail shadowing the cockpit. The headsail was taut, pulling the *Seabear* forward as we plowed through white-capped waves. It was going to be a nice day, finally some sunshine. Then I heard a loud bang. For a split second my view out the window was obscured by a flurry of white sails and metal – the sound was deafening, like fighter jets. The *Seabear* had righted herself and stopped. Blue sky and puffy clouds filled the cockpit window.

It all happened so fast: no warning signs, no long and drawn-out creaking noise. Just a loud bang, and in a matter of seconds the 70-foot mast was broken in half and down on the starboard side. The mainsail, headsail, all the rigging – everything now in the ocean. Then the shrieking sound of metal grinding against metal. The *Seabear* was wallowing back and fourth, adrift in the windswept sea. I went below deck and yelled, but everyone was up already, rushing through the companionway.

Time didn't slow; our lives didn't flash in front of us; there was no weird dreamlike quality to the scene. It was just very real. Visceral. Clear. So fucked up.

There was nothing we could do quickly; there was no fast remedy. We all slowed down and took it in: this mess, this disaster.

To me the solution seemed obvious: cut everything away and accept our losses. The shredded sails, the twisted rigging, the mast in two giant pieces banging against the hull. All of it was useless and extremely dangerous.

We cut a few things loose on deck, then Allen with mask and snorkel and knife in hand declared, "We're taking everything on board. It all goes with us!" And he jumped overboard. I couldn't believe what I'd heard. I watched him, amid whitecaps, slithering halyards, and massive pieces of broken mast, take a big breath through his snorkel and disappear.

Dave McGuire assesses the damage to the *Seabear*'s broken mast. Four hundred nautical miles short of Rapa Nui. Photo: Jeff Johnson

The *Seabear*'s crew emerges from the cockpit as Dave McGuire tends to the broken mast and captain Allen Szydlowski (in water) dives to salvage the remains. Four hundred nautical miles from Rapa Nui. Photo: Jeff Johnson

After four days of motoring, the disheveled *Seabear* arrived at Hanga Roa, Rapa Nui. With no adequate harbor and very little resources, captain Allen Szydlowski was forced to improvise. He referenced old plans sailors have used for centuries when they had to raise a mast while at sea. The cantilever system was complicated and dangerous. Rapa Nui. Photo: Jeff Johnson

The captain of the *Seabear*, Allen Szydlowski, fillets a mahi mahi. En route to Rapa Nui from the Galápagos Islands. Photo: Jeff Johnson

On deck we began the laborious and hazardous chore of cutting the rigging loose and organizing the mess to somehow get it all on board. Allen had been overboard and underwater for hours. He went through a couple of knives and a few pair of industrial scissors. I was still in disbelief. I couldn't understand why Allen wanted any of this wreckage.

We secured the pieces of mast against the hull, and Allen began cutting them into smaller ones. He stood on the broken mast sections, balanced there in the waves with an electric grinder. Every now and then he had to pull up to not get electrocuted by surging whitecaps. A few times he reacted too late, stiffened with his hair on end, and let out an involuntary yelp.

Once the mast was cut into smaller 15-foot chunks, we had to raise them over the railings; an engineering feat. We set up a complicated pulley system, using the forward windlass and the winches from inside the cockpit. It took hours of planning, careful execution, and full-on physical grunt work. The rough, rolling seas exaggerated the danger and difficulty of the work. To our amazement, by sundown we had everything onboard – the halyards coiled and tied down, the sails folded neatly, and the mast cut into four pieces and strapped to the gunwales. As the sun neared the horizon I looked over at Allen as he stood over the empty mast step, hands on his hips, his mind working overtime.

Now, a few days later, as I think through the whole debacle, I realize how lucky we were. If someone had been on deck when the mast came down he would have been killed. If this had happened at night, we would have had to deal with it in the dark. The danger factor would have tripled. It just so happened that the mast came down in the morning, with no one on deck, on a day when the wind was fading.

The culprit was a rear stay fitting. David McGuire, a friend and experienced captain who had been invited to join us on the crossing, showed me the fitting for the aft stay - one of the mainstays that hold up the mast. The halyard pulled right out of the fitting.

We're motoring now, listing back and fourth – a tiny, insignificant speck in the great Pacific Ocean, 304 nautical miles north of Easter Island. The merciless ocean shimmers like a sheet of wrinkled tinfoil. There is no object by which to mark our progress, no land, no vessel – just a blinking dot on the GPS and the sight of foam passing from the bow, running along the gunwales at five knots.

Yvon Chouinard once said, "It's not an adventure until something goes wrong." As much as I like this quote it has always bothered me in a way, robbing me of my own adventures.

But I reckon he is right.

Following spread: Rapa Nui is best known for its moai, which were toppled during the island's civil wars. Archaeologist Claudio Cristino restored some of the statues in the 1990s. Tongariki is the largest ahu on the Island. It includes 15 moai, among them an 86-ton moai that was the heaviest ever erected on the island. Ahu Tongariki, Rapa Nui. Photo: Jeff Johnson

RAPA NUI

The roosters wake up long before dawn. They're outside clawing the ground and calling for a sun that is three hours below the horizon. I fall asleep again. A couple of hours later, I'm startled by dogs barking, the muffled sound of four-stroke motorcycles, and horses trotting down the dirt road. I step out onto Makohe's lanai overlooking her garden and the town of Hanga Roa off in the distance. A thin trade wind rain dances in the sideways light as I weave through rows of plumeria and hibiscus. I start my borrowed Honda XL 175 and head into town.

I reach a bluff overlooking the small panga harbor in Hanga Roa and check the waves at Papa – the main surf spot in town. Nearly a mile outside the surf, the wounded *Seabear* wallows at anchor. Without a mast she looks naked, vulnerable, barely hanging on. Rapa Nui has no proper anchorages for boats *Seabear*'s size, so she remains anchored offshore. Allen and Kari's endurance amazes me. For 20 days now they have diligently worked on the boat to reconstruct a mast out of the scraps. They have come to shore only a few times.

I ride slowly through the small town and pull over next to a park on the corner of the main thoroughfare. Men are riding to work on horseback; horse hooves clack on the odd-shaped, dirt-colored bricks. The men's long, dark hair is tied into topknots. They wear plaid flannel shirts and army pants, and have machetes strapped to their waists. Women are riding triple on motorbikes, their flowered mu'umu'us tucked in between them, laughing and swaying through the traffic. The town has a large population of homeless dogs, but they look well-groomed and well-fed. German shepherds, collies, Labradors, ridgebacks, and pit bulls prance through the streets with big dog smiles and dripping red tongues. As the morning bustle simmers down, I head out of town to the desolate and rugged south coast.

There is an ever-present feeling of isolation here. One half of the horizon is always ocean, the other half, barren low-lying hills. It's the most remote habitable land on earth and possesses an eerie quietude like nothing else I've experienced. Even the strong, pervasive trade winds are silent as they caress the uneven landscape of black lava rock and weeds. I sit quietly next to a fallen moai statue at Akahanga. The statue lies face down in the dirt, its red *pakuo* – a volcanic rock headdress – rolled onto the grass when competing tribes toppled it hundreds of years ago. Increasingly, I'm drawn to these fallen moai; they represent a key element in the island's dark yet fascinating history.

It's a story that begins with a completely isolated, technologically advanced society and ends with environmental devastation brought on by this same society. Jared Diamond, in his book *Collapse: How Societies Choose to Fail or Succeed,* calls it the worst example of environmental destruction in the Pacific, and perhaps the world. Modern Easter Islanders are not proud of this. Instead, they celebrate the ingenuity it took for their ancestors to build the moai.

I first came to Akahanga with Makohe. On subsequent visits to the south coast we invariably ended up at Tongariki, where she would dance hula and sing next to the row of standing moai. But here, as we approached one of the many that had been toppled, she was unusually quiet. With her head hanging low, she stopped just short of the *ahu* and the row of fallen moai, massive ancient artifacts face down in the dirt, their proud grins turned upside down – the decimated, enigmatic keepers of long-kept secrets. No words were needed. Makohe's eyes said it all as she peered out across the white-capped ocean to the ever-increasing origin of nothingness.

A lone moai. Ahu Tongariki, Rapa Nui. Photo: Jeff Johnson

MAKOHE AND THE MOAI

We lie on the dirt, in the dark, next to a moai statue. Makohe sings. Like water, her soft voice permeates all that surrounds us – the cracks in the dry earth, the tight spaces between lava rocks, and the heavy aura of the standing moai of Tongariki. She sings in Hawaiian and in her native Rapa Nui tongue. She rests her hand on the side of the moai, lightly caressing the rough lava texture that has been broken down over centuries. I smell the raw earth, the salt in the air, and stare up at unfamiliar constellations, the Southern Cross tilted on its side dipping slowly toward a dark, infinite horizon.

Makohe and I had met a few days ago at the base of an ahu at Vinapu – a sacred platform at the top of a long, grassy slope that gave way to a cliff and an endless, windswept sea. She recounted stories of her childhood on Rapa Nui as she scanned the horizon, her dark brown eyes narrowing, as if the image in her memory might have appeared outlined on the ocean. She talked in a stream of consciousness, one unrelated story after another. There was a sense of poetry to her words: quick, uninhibited, and innocent.

"I used to see these pictures of my dad," she said. "They were in black and white. Our TV is all black and white. They always talk about *el continente*, the mainland. 'Oh, how is el continente?' And I always thought: black and white. I had that in mind because everything here is in color. I was used to blue ocean, white clouds, green grass. The first time I flew to the continent it was all color! I couldn't believe it; the people were in color too, like me."

"When I was little girl," she continued, "I never really had a doll. I mostly played outside, climbing trees and playing in the ocean. One day I found the head of a Barbie doll in the garbage. So I put it on a stick. That was my doll."

A face carved out of black lava peered out of the grass in front of us. A relic buried over time, its cavernous eyes staring blankly up to the sky. She said quietly, under her breath, "My ancestor…" I wondered what it might have been like to be raised here – surrounded by the past, the history of your people, their ancient faces and omnipresent stares – on the most remote island on earth.

Then, out of the blue, Makohe said, "I dreamt once that I was climbing with big shoes, the shoes that hook to the snow." She made a hacking motion with her hands that resembled ice climbing and continued. "I've never seen the ice before, but I knew I was safe. I was with friends."

I hadn't yet told her our plans. That we were sailing down to Patagonia in part to climb, and that this climbing required "big shoes that hook to the snow." Her dream may have been a clairvoyant rendering of fate. I don't know what possessed me, but I described our plans, and without thinking, asked if she wanted to join us. She wasn't surprised, but didn't reply with a yes or a no. Somehow I knew she would come with us.

Previous spread: Tehai on Rapa Nui's northwest shore is one of the island's premier but fickle big-wave venues.
Makohe Acuna and Jeff Johnson surfed this day, five days after Keith Malloy surfed the same swell at Mavericks in California. Tehai, Rapa Nui. Photo: Jeff Johnson

Makohe Acuna, injured from surfing Tehai, had stitches in her hip and a collection of deep abrasions. Rapa Nui. Photo: Jeff Johnson

Jeff Johnson finds a rare chunk of consolidated lava to climb. Mataveri, Rapa Nui. Photo: Tyler Emmett

Moai statues at the base of Rano Raraku quarry, Rapa Nui. The stone faces were carved from the slopes of the crater, released and slid to the base, where they were erected and prepared for transport. Rapa Nui. Photo: Jeff Johnson

Ahu Tongariki, Rapa Nui. Photo: Jeff Johnson

The base of an ahu (platform for moai statues). The masonry, similar to that used by the Inca, lends support to the late Thor Heyerdahl's highly controversial theory that the people of Rapa Nui came from South America. Vinapu, Rapa Nui. Photo: Jeff Johnson

ALGARROBA, CHILE

The passage from Rapa Nui to Juan Fernández – the island that inspired the book *Robinson Crusoe* – was one of the most enjoyable yet. We were blessed with sunny skies and calm seas, but it was sad to have to motor-sail the *Seabear* in her present state with a jury-rigged mast and sails.

The passage between Juan Fernández and mainland Chile was an entirely different story. For three days we wallowed at a painfully slow pace through unorganized chop and unpredictable winds. The conditions were so horrendous that on the radio we heard that two sailboats in a race had sunk, with all hands lost at sea. Everyday existence was miserable. Getting around below deck was like walking through a fun house at the carnival. I barely saw Allen and Kari. Makohe was sick the entire time, rarely coming out from her bunk.

Around 8 am on a Saturday, we motored into the calm waters of the marina at Algarroba. Kids in tiny sailboats tacked swiftly around the harbor. Stuffy, well-to-do families were boarding their perfectly clean yachts for day cruises, never hoisting the sails. As we were tying up to the dock, a family motored by us very slowly, almost touching. All of them were on deck, dressed in their best clothes, quietly staring at us as we adjusted the *Seabear* into position – tying lines off to cleats, hanging fenders, all of us shirtless, unshaven, and dirty.

The *Seabear* had a disheveled but proud look to her, as if she had just returned from battle. Metal railings bent and folded, an entire section missing along the port side, large dents in her steel hull where the broken mast had banged into her while we hauled it aboard, rust streaks dripping from the cracked paint, and the half stump of a mast jury-rigged with cut and sewn sails.

I waved to the family of "sailors" and said "*Hola.*" No one waved back or said a word.

It was the first time the *Seabear* had stopped rolling or bouncing in three months. It was strange not to feel her moving beneath our feet. We sat around the table in the main cabin recounting the passage. We'd been at it for 16 long days. The conversation drifted to ice cream, hot lattes, and dry, solid land. All of this lay just outside at the end of the dock, but no one made the effort to move. It was as if we expected more. But there wasn't. This was it.

So, we did what you are supposed to do after such a voyage. We all took naps and then went to the discotheque that night and got wasted.

Previous spread: Becalmed aboard the *Seabear*. After 36 days on Rapa Nui, the *Seabear* left Hanga Roa with a new crew member, Makohe Acuna. With a mast half its original height made from scraps and the sails cut down and sewn to fit, the only option was to motor sail the next 2,300 miles to mainland Chile. En route to mainland Chile. Photo: Jeff Johnson

Isla Juan Fernández lies off the coast of Chile. The island inspired the book *Robinson Crusoe*. Isla Juan Fernández, Chile. Photo: Jeff Johnson

RAMÓN NAVARRO

All the restaurants north of Pichilemu were closed. Our favorite spot was open but reserved for a private party. Chris, Danny, and I stood on the sidewalk out front wondering where to eat. Out came a well-dressed American who asked if we'd like to come inside and join the party. We'd been on the beach all day, surfing and lying around in the sand; we were a bit dirty and underdressed. Reluctantly we followed him in.

Once inside the man offered us fine wine, assorted cheeses, and a tableful of delectable fish hors d'oeuvres. He said he was holding a community meeting, getting the local surfers together with a politician who was running for mayor. It dawned on us that this was the Californian who had reportedly bought the biggest undeveloped portion of Punta de Lobos – Chile's crown jewel of surfing. It was rumored that he wanted to develop it and build condos, an underground parking lot, electric gates, fences – the works. The locals don't want the point to be developed that way and have already threatened him. This meeting was part of a strategic plan for the Californian to align himself with people of influence. We suddenly felt embarrassed to be at the dinner party, our consciences even dirtier than our clothes.

The calling from our empty stomachs overruled our guilt as we stood in the corner stuffing our faces. A few glasses of wine later, Ramón walked in wearing a traditional Mapuche poncho. We wanted to hide, but he saw us and walked up to us, smiling.

"Hey," he said. "What are you guys doing here?" He looked a little embarrassed as well.

"What are *you* doing here?" I laughed.

Then Chris leaned into him and whispered, "Keep your friends close, but keep your enemies closer."

Ramón, the son of a fisherman, was conceived in a tiny fishing shack perched at the top of Punta de Lobos overlooking the morros and his father's favorite fishing hole. His parents imparted to him their work ethic and knowledge of how to earn a living from nature: fishing, diving, and farming. And although he has become one of Chile's prominent big-wave riders and surfed around the world, he has maintained a connection to his homeland.

His father had watched the ocean change when big commercial fishing companies came in and destroyed the local fisheries. Ramón sees things changing also and has become one of the area's leading activists.

A few years ago a project was underway to put a sewage pipe out through the surf in his hometown of Pichilemu. Ramón refers to it as the "shit pipe." In an effort to stop it, he organized the local surfers and fishermen to pick all the trash off the beach and deliver

Previous spread: After parting ways with the Seabear, *Makohe Acuna and Jeff Johnson catch a rising south swell at Punta Lobos. Pichilemu, Chile. Photo: Jeff Johnson*

In the 1970s, Ramón's parents lived hand-to-mouth on the point overlooking the morros and his father's favorite fishing hole.
When Ramón was born they moved into a house down the beach near Pichilemu. His parents' shack, where Ramón is sitting, is long gone,
but Ramón (Chile's premier big-wave rider) has carried on with the family tradition of fishing and farming. Punta de Lobos, Pichilemu, Chile. Photo: Jeff Johnson

it to the mayor's house. The mayor was shocked to see truckloads of garbage dumped on his front yard. I was told Ramón, in a fit of protest, threw trash in the mayor's face. The shit pipe was stopped.

Back at the restaurant, the politician arrived late. He took off his coat and began his speech. Pacing the restaurant with swooping arms and a polished smile, he talked about progress: jobs, vacation homes, big industry, tourism. The vibe in the air was heavy. Something was going to go down. The three of us felt out of place – this was not our deal – so we went out back and sat by a fire pit overlooking the beach.

Inside, Ramón sat quietly and listened to what the politician had to say. When the man was done Ramón began to talk quietly, his voice getting stronger as he stood up. Looking through the window I saw Ramón, in his hooded poncho, approach the politician. He spread his arms wide and gestured toward the beach, pointed out to sea and then put a finger in the politician's face. The crowd was silent. I could hear Ramón's strong voice from where we sat.

The gringo landowner, realizing that the dinner party was a bad idea, tried to intervene. Ramón finished his speech, threw his hands in the air, and walked outside to join us. Everyone in the restaurant followed Ramón, leaving the politician and the landowner standing there

alone, speechless. In a huff, the politician walked out the door and drove away.

Ramón sat by us and placed his hands calmly over the fire. He talked about a coastal valley just to the south called Constitución. It houses the biggest pulp mill in the country.

"In the fifties," he said, "Constitución was one of the most culturally rich places in Chile. But when the cellulose mill came, it killed everything. It killed the fish. It killed the town. It killed the soul of the town. Cellulose waste is pumped right into the ocean. The whole coast is contaminated now."

He looked out into the darkness toward the sea. His eyes drifted off as he gathered his thoughts. He continued, "I see what happens when the people come with money and change … everything. We don't want to change the best and most beautiful place we have. And we're gonna fight for that, man."

Ramón's father, Alejandro Navarro, at home. Pichilemu, Chile. Photo: Scott Soens

Punta de Lobos, Pichilemu, Chile. Photo: Scott Soens

One of Chile's largest pulp mills sits above the beach. Constitución, Chile. Photo: Jeff Johnson

One of three toxic pointbreaks in Constitución, Chile. Constitución hosts one of Chile's largest pulp mills, situated between the town and the beach.
The cellulose mill produces waste that contains toxins such as dioxins and furans, which are toxic byproducts from bleaching and processing wood into the raw materials
used for consumer products such as paper, pulp, and lumber. The liquid and solid waste is dumped via pipeline into the local surf.
The three pointbreaks in Constitución are rarely, if ever, surfed because of the obvious health hazards. Constitución, Chile. Photo: Jeff Johnson

This page: A crab fisherman. Near the town of Cobquecura, Chile. Photo: Jeff Johnson
Previous spread: Abalone fisherman. Iglesia de Piedra near Cobquecura, Chile. Photo: Jeff Johnson

Jeff Johnson. Iglesia de Piedra near Cobquecura, Chile. Photo: Scott Soens

Crab fishermen. Cobquecura, Chile. Photo: Jeff Johnson

This page: Crab fishermen pull in their morning catch. Near the town of Cobquecura, Chile. Photo: Jeff Johnson
Following spread: Working their way south along the coast to Puerto Montt, Makohe Acuna and Jeff Johnson meet up with Keith Malloy near the town of Cobquecura. Chile. Photo: Jeff Johnson

THE RAPIDS OF RIO NEGRO

The last time I saw Keith – four months ago – he was wide-eyed and exhausted in Yosemite after we had climbed the North America Wall. In the time since, he had ridden the biggest wave of his life at Mavericks and had knee surgery - a direct result of the NA Wall. As we met up again he said he hadn't surfed in six weeks. It had been awhile for me as well.

Keith and I spent the next week surfing the long, pristine pointbreaks south of central Chile. The swell had been substantial but dissipated as we made our way south. In the city of Puerto Montt we hired a van and a driver to take us farther south into the ever-confusing roadways and ferry routes. We arrived at the port town of Horno Perrin, the end of the road where the land begins to break apart into fjords and bays forming the region of Patagonia. The tide was out and all the fishing boats lay on their sides in the muddy flats of an opaque, blue bay. Our next mode of transport, an old fishing boat named the *Cahuelmo*, was nowhere to be seen. We were told it would not arrive for another day or two.

That afternoon Keith and I stood on a bridge, covered head to toe in 5 mm neoprene, overlooking the rapids of the Rio Negro. We were quiet, mesmerized by the constant turmoil as the ice melt rushed over large boulders and dropped into deep, swirling holes. The cobalt-blue water looked inviting.

Keith and I are not river people, we're surfers. The only way for us to interpret the nature of these rapids was to compare them to ocean waves. The obvious difference here was that these waves never dissipated, whereas ocean waves have a definitive beginning and end. I had vaguely heard of river ratings before and told Keith that this was probably Class 1. We laughed about it; we both knew I had no idea what I was talking about.

Keith had brought down to Chile two 12'6" Joe Bark paddleboards. Awkwardly long, and narrow in width, they are tippy in turbulent water. Made of thin fiberglass, they definitely aren't meant to come into contact with hard objects like granite boulders. Walking through the lush forest with the boards under our arms, I had a hard time accepting the fact that we were about to paddle prone down a river. The excitement built in my stomach, as though I were about to paddle out to some secret big-wave spot in Northern California.

In the distance the baritone drone of the river mimicked the sound of gigantic waves. A thick canopy of trees blocked out the sun. The closeness of the vine-wrapped trees made them difficult to negotiate; we had to bush-whack our way to the river's edge. Like two clumsy drunks emerging from a dark bar in the middle of the day, Keith and I stepped out of the jungle into the bright light and halted. Whitewater everywhere, its roar much louder than our voices. Pockets of mist undulated in the crisp, ionized air. We looked at each other and laughed again.

Rio Negro near the town of Horno Perrin. Patagonia, Chile. Photo: Jeff Johnson

Keith Malloy riding the biggest wave of his life. Maverick's, California. Photo: Jeff Flindt

Keith jumped in and I followed. He immediately pointed upstream and paddled like hell as he tried to catch and surf a standing wave. Instead he just flew through the initial rapids backwards. I careened by him and tried to shoot a gap between two boulders that led to the roughest section, the one I had seen from the bridge. The next thing I knew I was dry-docked on a huge chunk of granite surrounded by whitewater. I had slid up there, board and all, and broke off the fin. I slid back down the rock and spun backwards through the gap into the hissing turmoil. Keith was ahead of me again, appearing and disappearing between mounds of water. I had very little control now that my fin was gone. All I could do was hold on and take a few awkward strokes here and there. Then, as quickly as it all began, we passed under the bridge into calmer water. The noise of the rapids faded in the distance as Keith and I floated effortlessly through soft riffles made golden by the descending sun.

We had made camp a mile or so down the river. The plan was for our taxi driver to send someone out and flag us in to camp. We didn't know where this take-out spot was and we were in wild, unfamiliar terrain. We drifted on.

We saw no one. It got dark. Keith and I floated on, moving swiftly with the constant flow of water. We didn't know what to do. All rivers end in the ocean, so maybe we would end up there.

I rolled off my board and thanks to my thick wetsuit, floated on my back without effort. I lay there with my limbs spread out wide, weightless like an astronaut floating in outer space. Stars rotated above like tiny pinholes of light in a canopy of black velvet. A crescent moon rose over the silhouetted ridgeline to the north.

This journey, traveling to Chile by boat, has led me far off the beaten path. The extended stay on Rapa Nui had been the turning point for me as I finally let go of the trappings from my life back home – a slow and difficult process. But it was here – floating in a river on the very edge of Patagonia – that I realized home is not a physical reference to a specific place on earth, but a broadening of the consciousness. Home is, after all, where you are.

It was nearly midnight as we passed from the river to the ocean. Floating in the brackish water, I savored the familiar taste of salt, the pungent smell of sea life. Standing in muddy tidal flats of a large bay, we could see the dim lights of a town no less than two miles away. With our huge paddleboards we walked for what seemed like hours.

Following spread: Keith Malloy finds solitude on empty point waves north of Puerto Montt, Chile. Photo: Devon Howard

REÑIHUÉ

The *Cahuelmo* motors south with Makohe, Keith, and me aboard. We are going to visit Doug and Kris Tompkins at their compound in Reñihué. I have never met the two of them and have seen Doug only in the obscure film *Mountain of Storms*. I have heard so much about both of them, though, that it feels as if I know them personally.

Kris had worked in the mailroom for Yvon Chouinard after school and during the summers. She worked her way up to CEO of Patagonia by the time she was 28 and stayed on for 15 years before she left to join Doug in Chile.

In the 1960s, Doug – a high school dropout – started a mountain shop called The North Face. With the profits from the sale he and his first wife, Susie Tompkins Buell, founded the clothing company Esprit, which eventually reached sales of a billion dollars a year before the Tompkinses separated and sold the business.

In 1992, Doug purchased a Yosemite-sized piece of temperate rainforest in southern Chile. He and Kris set up base in Reñihué, on the ocean edge of the property, restored the land to its natural state, named the 762,000-acre property Parque Pumalín, and opened it to the public.

Today, Pumalín has worldwide significance. It combines large-scale wilderness protection, land restoration, and organic farming. It has become the world's largest privately owned land-conservation project. But this philanthropic endeavor has not been without controversy. Chilean nationalists accused the Tompkinses of ulterior motives ranging from spearheading a geographical breakup of Chile, to the creation of a CIA spy station, to the founding of a Zionist enclave (although neither Kris nor Doug is Jewish).

Doug has remained unwavering in his political ideals and deep ecology philosophy, which holds, in part, that human consumption must be reduced to restore the planet's health.

He says, "We humans are doing nothing more than manufacturing our own coffins in space. The ecosystem can only tolerate so much. We're consuming like there's no tomorrow."

The Chileans, after many years of debate, have finally recognized the fact that the Tompkinses are protecting Chile's natural resources. Finally, in August 2006, the Chilean government ended its long battle over Pumalín by granting it official protected status and promising to convert it to a national park.

Onboard the *Cahuelmo*, the expanse of Golfo de Ancud has tightened as we enter the narrow fjord of Reñihué. The sky is abnormally cloudless for these parts, the water calm, and the air eerily still. The muffled gurgling sound of the *Cahuelmo*'s engine permeates the silence.

The Tompkinses' residence is accessible only by boat or small plane. Located at the base of the remote fjord, it is surrounded by lush jungle and flanked by white-capped mountains. None of the compound's buildings are visible as we climb out of the dingy. To our surprise, Yvon Chouinard – fly-fishing rod in hand – waits for us on the muddy tidal flats. He smiles and talks excitedly, mostly about fly fishing – his life-long obsession.

He leads us down a long gravel road lined with tall Norfolk pines. The compound, encompassed by rich foliage and trees, is comprised of low-lying, earth-colored structures. We pass an organic garden, comfortable living

One of the original structures in Reñihué, dubbed the "Hobbit's House." Doug Tompkins lived here for over a year when he first bought the land in 1992. There was no electricity and no running water. Reñihué, Chile. Photo: Jeff Johnson

Makohe Acuna and Keith Malloy aboard the *Cahuelmo*, entering the Reñihué fjord. Reñihué, Chile. Photo: Jeff Johnson

quarters for the employees – where we are to stay – and a machine shop/wood-working garage, and arrive at the Tompkinses' humble home. Everything is immaculate. The atmosphere is that of a Buddhist retreat. Doug has had direct influence on everything from the architecture of the buildings to the specific orientation of the toilet paper holders.

After dinner one evening, the Tompkinses invite us over to their home to watch a few DVDs about the parks. Before the viewing Doug talks candidly about his efforts and what has inspired him. He begins his speech with the word "love." The conclusions he draws from the word and its origins make perfect sense to me, but I can't help but be thrown off by this. It sounds so sensitive and esoteric coming from this seemingly tough and stoic revolutionary. "Love," he says, "is what it all boils down to."

In a section of one DVD subtitled "Sharing the Planet with Others," Doug quotes naturalist Lois Crisler: "… species of every ecosystem around the world are going extinct, not by the hour, but by the minute." In a stern and haunting voice, Doug makes clear which animals are near extinction.

"The huemul deer," he says. "The result of a billion years of evolution. Almost gone, forever. The giant river otter, eliminated from most of its habitat. Almost gone, forever. The tall and elegant maned wolf. Almost gone, forever."

As the night wanes, I am overwhelmed at the scope of their land preservation projects. What started as an experiment in land conservation in Reñihué has now turned into a string of national parks, which when combined cover almost 2 million acres. There's Parque Pumalín in northern Patagonia, consisting of 800,000 acres; Corcovado National Park just south of Pumalín, at 100,000 acres; and Monte Leone in southern Patagonia, with over 150,000 acres. They have a current project

in Corrientes Province in northern Argentina, where they have purchased 600,000 acres. And their newest, and most ambitious, effort is Valle Chacabuco, which comprises 170,000 acres. It's mind-boggling what Kris and Doug have set out as their life goal.

Keith spends one afternoon in the workshop shaping a new wooden fin for the paddleboard – the one I had broken and lost during our paddle down the river. A few days later we take the paddleboards out for a long voyage up the Reñihué fjord. The tide is low, but from the occasional surge pouring in over the mud flats we can see it is now filling in. The wind is dead calm; the air is crisp. We take our first lazy strokes out over the opaque, powder-blue shallows. There used to be a salmon farm here. Doug had gotten rid of it; he said it killed most of the life in the fjord, but now that life is slowly coming back.

Keith paddles ahead of me as we enter the deepest part of the channel. Up ahead we see a school of curious sea lions angling out to greet us. As we get closer to them a flock of cormorants appear, hovering just above our heads, screeching and flapping their wings. The sea lions dive and disappear. We paddle farther up the channel, the two of us gaining momentum through the dark, glassy water. Suddenly, we're startled by a ghostlike figure swimming beneath us. With perfect timing, as if choreographed, the dolphin jumps through the air between us, articulating perfect half-moon arcs. Then more appear, jumping and diving all around us. Keith and I sit up on our boards and are surrounded by eight dusky dolphins. They seem to be smiling and we can hear them squeaking below the surface. I pause and look up at the snowcapped peaks and gaze out over the fjord and the lush tangles of jungle spilling down to the water.

Like a tribal drum, Doug's voice thumps loudly in the base of my head, the words "Gone, forever."

Yvon Chouinard teaches Makohe Acuna to fly fish, with Keith Malloy in the background. Reñihué, Chile. Photo: Jeff Johnson

This page: Clams and limpets foraged at low tide in a sheltered cove. Reñihué, Chile. Photo: Jeff Johnson

Following spread: In Reñihué the crew met up with Timmy O'Neill and Yvon Chouinard to explore some of the unclimbed mountains in the region. The crew of five rendezvoused with the *Cahuelmo* in the town of Chaitén. From there they motored south to Cerro Corcovado. The *Cahuelmo* rests at low tide in a sheltered cove. The coast below Corcovado, Chile. Photo: Danny Moder

Previous spread: Timmy O'Neill organizes his climbing rack for the Corcovado climb, aboard the *Cahuelmo* in a sheltered cove. Below Corcovado, Chile. Photo: Jeff Johnson

This spread: Timmy O'Neill, Jeff Johnson, and Yvon Chouinard aboard the *Cahuelmo*, on their way to climb Corcovado. Patagonia, Chile. Photo: Scott Soens

Wild strawberries on the coast. Below Cerro Corcovado, Patagonia, Chile. Photo: Scott Soens

Keith Malloy heads out to a wave that had previously not been surfed. Having had his share of climbing on El Capitan in Yosemite, Keith opted to stay behind and search for unridden waves. The coast below Corcovado, Chile. Photo: Danny Moder

Keith Malloy enjoys the view of Corcovado. Patagonia, Chile. Photo: Frame grab from the film *180° South*

CORCOVADO ASCENT

Like feathers, the words came floating down through the cool, windless air, hovering just out of reach as I tried to discern their meaning. "If we continue, we have a fifty-fifty chance of dying."

I tried to repeat these words to understand them but was unable to. So I let them flutter past me, out over the cliff, and disappear into the folds of the glacier far below.

My position was precarious, like standing on the slanted roof of a high-rise building, in hard boots, on marbles. I had kicked out a step in the dirt for the belay – each kick sending a cascade of rocks over the 500-foot drop to my right. I could no longer see Timmy, but I knew his situation was worse. Before taking off on lead he put his face close to mine.

"Take a picture," he said with wide, crazy eyes, "'cause it might be the last time you see Timmy O'Neill alive." He made a few moves up the loose face, dislodging rocks of all sizes, which rolled over the edge. He stopped and looked at the coil of rope between my feet. "You might want to take a picture of yourself too. You're attached to me."

We had no anchor; we had no belay.

I stood there feeling naked. If Timmy were to fall he would tumble by me, then soar out over the glacier, at which point I'd see the 50 meters of coiled rope feed out in a matter of seconds. Then I'd be gone too, yanked off the mountain like a cartoon character – the two of us cartwheeling through the air. Timmy's footing gave way and he pitter-pattered his feet a little higher. A nervous laugh leapt from his throat. He moved on, slowly, and disappeared into an alcove above.

Then came those words. "If we continue, we have a fifty-fifty chance of dying."

"What?" I yelled back to him, stalling to let it sink in.

It had taken us three days to get high enough to see a possible approach to Cerro Corcovado: a 10-mile Zodiac ride up a river that ruined three outboard props, an all-day rock-hop up a labyrinth of winding rivers, and miles of horrible bushwhacking. Half the time we thought we were lost. Yvon commented more than once, "I'm getting too old for this shit." Eventually, we made high camp at the last of four pristine lakes where we thought no one had been before – unless they'd dropped in by helicopter or airplane.

Today we were up at 2 am to push for the summit. It took hours of bushwhacking in the dark to get to the glacier's base. Yvon hadn't slept well. Maybe he was over it. We sat on cold rocks surrounded by ice; I asked him when he last climbed a mountain.

He thought for a minute. "I don't know," he answered. "I can't remember."

His ice axe and crampons were more than 30 years old. He had made them himself, forged them in an old tin shed, the original headquarters for Chouinard Equipment Company. I watched him carefully lace his crampons, and as soon as they touched the ice his eyes lit up. He stood up quickly and studied the glacier with newfound intensity.

"The higher I get, the better I feel," he said, breathing in the cool, thin air. "Ah, to get up into the alpine world… it's the best." He made a few offhand remarks about

Yvon Chouinard, Makohe Acuna, and Timmy O'Neill approach the glacier on the morning of the summit attempt. Corcovado, Chile. Photo: Jeff Johnson

Timmy O'Neill, Yvon Chouinard, Jeff Johnson, and Makohe Acuna make the long approach to Cerro Corcovado. Patagonia, Chile. Photo: Danny Moder

climbing and dying, then bent over laughing. This didn't sit well with Makohe. She was on unfamiliar terrain. Raised on the most remote island on Earth, she had never climbed or seen ice; she'd seen snow only once.

We arrived at the top of the glacier to find that the last few pitches to the summit were rotten rock – red and black and brown in color. It looked too dangerous for Makohe, maybe too dangerous for anyone. Yvon sacrificed his chance for the summit and offered to help Makohe down the glacier. Timmy and I had to try.

The only person ever to stand on the top of Corcovado is Doug Tompkins. When he climbed it the summit was covered with ice and snow. We had arrived in the middle of the worst drought in some 20 years. Perfect weather, not a cloud in sight, no snow, no ice – only dry, rotten rock.

"If we continue, we have a fifty-fifty chance of dying." Timmy's words began to sink in. I could see lines of swell rolling through the strait in the ocean below, refracting off reefs, peeling down the coastline beneath us. Keith was down there, somewhere, riding waves. Suddenly I wanted to join him. I wanted to be off this thing.

"Come up and see for yourself!" Timmy yelled, his words like tiny fists jabbing me in the ribs. "Just don't weight the rope or the anchor might blow – then we both go!"

I didn't have to see for myself. I didn't want to see the next "fifty-fifty-chance-of-dying" pitch. I knew that two morons making one decision were worse than one moron. In a speech about alpinism, Yvon once commented on the current state of climbing Mount

Everest, where wealthy clients pay guides to get them to the top. He said, "You get to the top and there's nothing up there. If your primary goal is the summit, you are missing the whole point. The purpose of climbing is to effect some sort of spiritual and physical gain, but if you compromise the process, you're an asshole when you start out and you're an asshole when you get back."

We decided to bail. It took us two rappels to get back to the glacier. The first from a single, medium-sized cam stuffed awkwardly between two loose blocks, the second from two small cams dangling from a flared crack. Timmy wasn't saying much, and my stomach was in knots. I had thought about this climb for more than two years. Anxiety had built for months on the sail down here. And we were shut down, just like that.

Stepping from the glacier onto solid ground, Timmy tore off his gear as if ridding himself of some horrible disease. Surrounded by the brilliant light of a descending sun, Corcovado behind him and the ocean below, he leaned back with arms spread wide as if to hug all of life. I saw the tension fall from his face and form into a grin. Then he looked straight at me, put his finger to his lips, and blew the smoke from the end of his make-believe pistol.

Following spread: Timmy O'Neill near high camp. Cerro Corcovado, Chile. Photo: Jeff Johnson.

The crew at Camp II. Cerro Corcovado. Patagonia, Chile. Photo: Jimmy Chin

Timmy O'Neill leading the last pitch on Cerro Corcovado, just minutes before making the call to turn back. Photo: Jeff Johnson

Timmy O'Neill leading a fish out of water, Makohe Acuna, up Cerro Corcovado's glacier. Patagonia, Chile. Photo: Jeff Johnson

Facilitated by Conservación Patagónica, Corcovado is one of Chile's newest national parks. Photo: Jeff Johnson

CORCOVADO DESCENT

Backing off from our attempt on Corcovado we stepped off the glacier. As we descended back to camp, Timmy and I got separated. Darkness fell. Trees surrounded me. I lost my sense of direction. After climbing and dropping into consecutive gullies filled with boulders and bushes and trees, I began to admit that maybe I was lost. Was I covering the same ground over and over? I stopped and looked up at the black sky.

"Timmy!" I yelled. "Timmy!" No answer, not even an echo of my own voice.

Our high camp was on the black sand beach of a lake. If I could just make it to that sand I would be close. The rest would be easy. More gullies, more rocks and trees, and more horrible bushes. Whenever I squeezed past a bush, the rope I carried coiled around my neck would snag and then my boots hanging from my neck would punch me in the face. I began to take this personally. After the fiftieth beating, I snapped. Whirling around, I faced the offending bush, tore the boots from my neck, threw my rope to the ground, and yelled. "You bastard!" I beat the living shit out of that bush with my ice axe.

Eventually I found sand. I followed the familiar black sand and the multitude of dead tree stumps. I was getting close. I saw flickering light, the campfire. I turned and walked toward the light. A half hour later my boots punched me in the face again, and I stopped in a gulley surrounded by trees and bush.

Wasn't I just standing on the beach? Was I going crazy? I began to consider whether I had crossed into another dimension. I resigned myself to the fact that I was under the control of something I didn't understand and wandered aimlessly. The adrenaline from the climb had long ago drained away. Fatigue had set in. I'd been at it for over 20 hours now. I was tired and pissed off.

After what seemed like hours I came to some water: the lake. The moon had fully risen. I began to run toward the moon. But the darkness hid a three-foot-tall tree stump. It caught me in the crotch and I toppled head over heels in the sand. My boots punched me in the face; my rope got tangled around my feet.

"That's it." I threw my gear to the ground, raised my axe, and I beat the shit out of that one, too.

As I walked slowly by the water, contemplating the idea of being in another dimension, I noticed something shiny in the sand. As I got closer I wished it to be a can of beer. I could sure use a beer right now, I thought.

To my dismay it was. A can of *Escudo*. And then another can, and another. Ten cans of Escudo, just lying there in the sand. It's true, I thought. I've passed through to another dimension. I filled my arms with cans of beer and stood up awkwardly in the yellow glow of the moon. I accepted my destiny, and walked proudly by the lake's edge, downing the beer in large, noisy gulps.

Working on my second beer I was stopped in my tracks by the light of a fire, bodies sitting around it, people eating food, the sound of laughter. A man approached me.

"Jeff," said Timmy with concern. "Where have you been?"

I was silent, dumbfounded. He handed me a bottle of whiskey. "Here," he said. "Rodrigo flew by in his Husky this afternoon and dropped beers and whiskey for us. Have a shot." I had a pull from the bottle and sat down by the fire. Firelight flickered on the faces of my friends. I looked long and hard from one to the other, and wondered if they had any clue what the hell was going on.

Previous spread: The first of four pristine lakes on the approach to Cerro Corcovado. Patagonia, Chile. Photo: Jeff Johnson

Cerro Corcovado as seen from first high camp at the first of four lakes. Corcovado, Chile. Photo: Jimmy Chin

Jeff Johnson catches his first wave below Cerro Corcovado. Patagonia, Chile. Photo: Danny Moder

THE OFF-WIDTH

"There's something about pigeon-toed girls," Yvon said as he tied a fly to his leader, watching subtle ripples in the lake's edge out of the corner of his eye. "You know, the way a woman walks with her feet turned slightly in? It does something to her physique, her stride – really adds to it."

He finished tying on the fly and cast it out onto the lake. A silent, horizontal whip. "Oh, man," he said as he stripped it back in. "It's so damn sexy to me."

All the rock we had seen since Corcovado was complete choss – beautiful from a distance, but crumbly like kitty litter when touched. The rock around this lake was different, more solid. So I convinced Yvon that we should climb a crack across the lake.

Yvon was skeptical as we set up to rappel down the 200-foot wall to a hanging belay above the water. He couldn't remember the last time he climbed on rock. His shoes were ancient and he didn't own a harness.

"There's no way you're gonna hip-belay me, Yvon," I told him.

"What do you mean?" he said. "You'll be fine. It's safe."

I pulled out a borrowed harness and belay device and handed them to him. He took them begrudgingly, shook his head, and grunted.

I left Yvon at a belay 10 feet above the water. The rock was pretty rotten, but the surface was smooth inside the crack. As I climbed higher, the crack widened and I began shimmying inside the rotten off-width. I pulled off big chunks of rock and threw them into the water below. The splashes made a *thunk* that echoed from the other

wall across the lake. I searched deep inside the crack with my #4 Camalot, pulling and releasing the trigger, only to have it open into air, the lobes touching nothing.

"The gear is shitty up here," I yelled down to Yvon.

"What?" he said, the wind whipping his voice up the face.

I was taking forever. Yvon hunkered down on the tiny ledge, slouching over with his head down while tiny pebbles rained on him. Eventually, I got in an okay piece of protection. The off-width arched out above me, overhanging and flared, the rock just as rotten. I had two rickety pieces of protection in the last 50 or 60 feet. A fall could have been disastrous. I aided the next 15 feet to a good belay stance and made an anchor behind a large, detached block. Better than nothing, I said to myself.

"Yvon!" I yelled. "You're on!"

Slowly and calmly, Yvon cleaned the belay and leaned against the wall. Then he sank his arm into the crack – a strong fist inside that dark, deteriorated sandstone. He leaned out from the wall and dissected the climb with sharp, gleaming eyes. The golden years of his Yosemite rock climbing came boiling to the surface. Yvon dug into that wall like a dancing pit bull – aggressive but elegant – shimmying through the off-width with perfect technique and precision. Climbers today avoid off-widths. In Yvon's heyday they sought them out and mastered them. Nearly every Yosemite first ascent in his day had one. And I witnessed a 69-year-old veteran show how it's done.

Yvon paused at the rotten, overhanging section I had aided. He traversed out of the crack and worked through a series of strenuous face moves. He fell onto my belay a

Previous spread: After their attempt on Cerro Corcovado the crew regrouped back in Chaitén and made plans to visit Kris Tompkins' new future national park in Valle Chacabuco. In Chaitén they procured an old truck and spent two days driving south on dirt and gravel roads. Jeff Johnson passed out after hours on the road. Valle Chacabuco, Chile. Photo: Danny Moder

few times, but kept going until thoroughly spent. Finally, he threw some prusiks on the rope and ascended the last 15 feet to the belay. He breathed heavily in the dying light. I suggested we prusik the rest of the way up our fixed line, but Yvon scanned the wall for other possibilities.

"Look," he said pointing. "That crack to our left. That'll go."

A small crack ran up a right-facing dihedral, and before I could even think about it Yvon said, "Give me the rack."

Yvon had to traverse 25 feet across a sloping, sandy ledge to reach the dihedral. He stood above me with a #.75 Camalot, opening and closing it, and stared at it like it was some object from outer space. I realized he had never used one before. He plugged it blindly behind a loose block and continued the traverse.

He arrived at the dihedral and began to stem the corner – a difficult move for anyone. Lifting himself up, he tried to match his left foot to his left hand. I watched in horror as he just barely tickled the edge of the hold with his toe – his leg shaking, his hips cramping.

Twice he began to fall backwards and twice he caught himself. A fall would pendulum him across the wall, pull out the cam, dislodge the block above me, and result in a fall on my not-so-good anchor. On the third try he stuck it and stood in the corner. The sun lowered and the warm alpenglow turned the rock around us a pinkish orange. Yvon was in his own world, totally confident.

He pulled out another cam and shoved it casually into the crack. The lobes just flapped open and it hung there without purchase.

"Is that a good piece?" I yelled to him.

"Yep," he said, and quickly stemmed the corner again and began to lie-back the crack, walking his feet up the wall.

None of the pieces he had put in were good. His generation's ethic was that you just don't fall. Yvon found a good stance and plunged in another piece. This one was good; finally, I could breathe. He quickly climbed the last of the crack and disappeared over the top.

A minute later he said, "You're on."

Our timing was perfect. We still had enough light to make it to the road. I looked back across the lake – the entire sky turning blood red – at the awkward, less-than-perfect off-width we had just groveled on.

"Yvon," I said into the quiet desert air. "I've always had a thing for girls with a lazy eye."

"Huh?" he asked with a puzzled look.

"You know, she's looking at you, but one eye is slightly askew and you're trying to figure out which eye to look at?" I replied.

"Ha!" he laughed, "yeah, yeah."

"There's something humble about it," I said. "It's a peculiar kind of beauty – sexy and cute at the same time. I'm a sucker for it."

Yvon moved slowly, studying each foot as it played out before him, one careful step at a time. Here and there he would let out a quiet laugh and shake his head as if in agreement to something he'd been pondering forever.

Following spread: The off-width above an unnamed lake in Argentina on the Chilean border. Near Valle Chacabuco, Patagonia, Chile. Photo: Danny Moder

CERRO GEEZER

For 10 years now, Doug and Yvon have been eyeing what they call "Cerro Geezer." It's an unnamed, unclimbed mountain located on the northern margin of the Valle Chacabuco, which Kris Tompkins, Doug's wife, had purchased as the centerpiece of the future Patagonia National Park. When completed, the park will consist of 173,000 acres. Maybe this year, Yvon had said, Cerro Geezer will finally give way to a "geriatric ascent."

Last year Yvon and Doug gave it a go but were immediately thwarted by technical difficulties. Ten steps into the long approach, Yvon's 30-year-old mountain boots shattered. With the peak no longer an option, they embarked on a long and arduous hike back to Valle Chacabuco.

This year they have decided to give it another try and asked me to tag along. I eagerly agreed. Aside from that horrendous off-width Yvon and I climbed beside a lake in Argentina, I have never been part of a first ascent. And I didn't want to miss a chance to climb with two legendary "geezers."

My mountaineering experience is very limited. My attempt with Timmy on Corcovado was the first time I had put on crampons or used an ice axe. But I've read a lot about mountaineering. If a climbing story is in print, then something bad happened. As a result, I have read nothing but stories involving mountaineering disasters. I can only expect the worst. And I have dressed accordingly: heavy-duty water-resistant pants, long underwear, fleece, a waterproof shell, synthetic

puffy jacket packed neatly away, gloves, glacier glasses – the works.

All dressed up, I leaned against my large backpack, waiting for Doug to get ready. I didn't realize that Doug had been ready all along. He shouldered his small pack and walked past me wearing the same clothes he'd had on all morning: pleated cotton slacks, a cashmere sweater worn over a pressed collared shirt, and a white golf hat. His tennis shoes where exactly that – designed for tennis, not hiking. They were pure white and spotless.

Everyone has his or her own pace. Mine is a bit fast. Yvon's pace is slow and steady. I had assumed that, Doug being close to Yvon's age, his pace would also be slow. I forced myself to slow down so I could spend time with these guys. To my amazement, Doug was off and, almost literally, running. I couldn't keep up. Out of breath, I asked Yvon about Doug's speedy pace. He said Doug had always been that way – fast. It had been the same on all their climbs: the tortoise and the hare. I looked up ahead as Doug, prancing like a gazelle, scrambled up loose scree and jumped over some large talus, his lanky figure dwarfed by Cerro Geezer.

Yvon lowered his voice and said in all seriousness, "I think he's a little nervous."

"Why's that?" I asked.

"Over the past few years Doug has developed heart arrhythmia. The medication he was on was making it

This page: Doug Tompkins and Yvon Chouinard near the top of the upper glacier. Cerro Geezer, Patagonia, Chile. Photo: Jeff Johnson
Following spread: Yvon Chouinard and Doug Tompkins descend from high camp the day after their summit of Cerro Geezer,
which Doug has renamed Cerro Kristine, after his wife, Kris Tompkins. Cerro Kristine, Patagonia, Chile. Photo: Jeff Johnson

Yvon Chouinard wakes up at high camp. Cerro Geezer, Chile. Photo: Danny Moder

worse. His new medication seems to be working better though. I think he's a bit nervous about this climb and what it might do to him."

Yvon was quiet and contemplative with this thought. Then he cupped his hand around his mouth and yelled toward him, "Dead man walking. Ha, ha. We got a dead man walking here."

It took the better part of the day to get to high camp. On a wide ridge beside a glacier, we traded stories over dinner tucked behind a windbreak we'd made from rocks as the sun dropped into the corner of a hard, cloudless sky.

We arrived at the upper reaches of the glacier the next morning, just as the sun glanced around the northern flanks of the Geezer. We climbed near-vertical ice to reach a ridge, which brought us to the base of a technical rock-climbing section. I took off my pack, brought out a 50-meter rope and a small rack, and asked Yvon if we should rope up.

He looked over at me with a smirk. "Every man for himself," he laughed, and took off up the first pitch of rock. Doug was already up there, free climbing in his golfing outfit. I followed Yvon over the first easy slab that gave way to an exposed buttress.

In the early afternoon we reached the shoulder that lead to the summit. Just below the summit blocks, Doug stopped and stepped to the side. In his typical, gentlemanly fashion, he gestured for me to pass.

"Here you go," he said. He knew I had never made a first ascent. "It's all yours."

I stopped, Yvon standing behind me. "Go ahead," said Yvon. "Go for it."

I looked up at the virgin peak, the clear blue sky, and the vast wilderness of mountains, glaciers, and rivers that surrounded it. We were three insignificant souls on the precipice of wonder.

Doug and Yvon had eyed this mountain for 10 years and had already failed on one attempt. There was no way I was going to accept their offer. "It's yours, Doug. You go."

With not a cloud in the sky, we had a 360-degree view of the world around us. From the foot of the Geezer pressing outward was an endless array of unclimbed, unexplored peaks and valleys. Standing proud to the south was Cerro San Lorenzo, one of the tallest, most remote mountains in Patagonia. To the west, beyond the Rio Baker, lay the Northern Patagonia Icefield and Monte San Valentin, the highest mountain in South America south of 40 degrees.

Doug took in a big breath of air. "Feels good, doesn't it," he said to me.

"Yeah," I said. "It sure does. What are you going to call it?"

Doug looked out over the world, lost in thought. Then he quietly said, "Cerro Kristine. Cerro Kristine. I think she would like that."

Dark clouds filled the sky as we prepared dinner back at high camp. Doug and Yvon related one epic story after another. They've had countless adventures together. They argue at times, call each other on their bullshit, but it's all done with deep affection. It's a bond similar to one that comes from years of marriage, but in their case, it comes from sharing a multitude of near-death experiences.

Yvon and I curled up in our bivy sacks under a dark, ominous sky. Doug slept in a tent. In the middle of the night I felt a light drizzle on my face. The drizzle turned to rain. In a fitful sleep I noticed my down-feather sleeping bag was getting soggy, so I crawled into the tent with Doug.

We woke in the morning to a peculiar quality of light inside the tent, dull and colorless. Doug reached a hand up and flicked his finger against the ceiling. A chunk of snow dropped away and some light poured in. Doug's eyes sparkled. "Ooh, that's a lot of snow."

"Yvon!" I yelled. "How ya doing out there?" We heard crunching sounds coming from Yvon's bivy sack and a few muffled groans.

Doug could barely contain his excitement. "There might be too much snow to get the car out," he said. "We left it at a pretty high elevation. We're going to have to hike out of here via Valle Furioso. There is water down there and we can find wood to make a fire. From there we can hike back to Chacabuco."

"How long will that take?" I asked.

Doug thought about it. "About three days."

Three days, I thought. We were already on our third day and I was beat. That would mean six days for the whole trip. Then, from outside the tent, among soft crunching noises, we heard Yvon grunt, "That's bullshit!"

A few days later, the three of us sat near the Rio Chacabuco, sipping maté beneath the shade of poplar trees. In the distance, below a mass of cotton-ball clouds, stood Cerro Kristine, resplendent in the setting sun.

"How do you two do it?" I asked Doug and Yvon. "Most people your age aren't climbing mountains and they tend to get more conservative in their political ideals – all that radical stuff just a phase they went through."

After a long pause – as with all questions I had asked – Doug answered, "Don't hang out with old people." They laughed. Then Yvon, slapping his knee, chimed in, "Always make sure you are the oldest person in the room."

This page: Doug Tompkins at high camp. Cerro Geezer, Patagonia, Chile. Photo: Jeff Johnson
Following spread: Yvon Chouinard at high camp. Cerro Geezer, Chile. Photo: Danny Moder

Jeff Johnson, Doug Tompkins, and Yvon Chouinard on the summit of Cerro Geezer. Patagonia, Chile. Photo: Frame-grab from the film *180° South*

Yvon Chouinard mantles the summit ridge. Cerro Geezer, Patagonia, Chile. Photo: Jeff Johnson

THE CREW

The crew on location. Corcovado coast, Patagonia, Chile. Photo: Jimmy Chin

Yvon Chouinard. Valle Chacabuco, Chile. Photo: Scott Soens

Kris and Doug Tompkins. Valle Chacabuco, Chile. Photos: Scott Soens

Chris Malloy. Corcovado coast, Chile. Photo: Scott Soens

Keith Malloy. Corcovado coast, Chile. Photo: Scott Soens

Jeff Johnson. Valle Chacabuco, Chile. Photo: Scott Soens

Rick Ridgeway. Valle Chacabuco, Chile. Photo: Scott Soens

Producer Tim Lynch and Makohe Acuna. Valle Chacabuco, Chile. Photos: Scott Soens

Cinematographer Tyler Emmett completed the entire trip along with Jeff Johnson from Ixtapa, Mexico, to Chacabuco, Patagonia.
A one-man band, he was the key element in everything from film production to the actual adventure. His job descriptions ranged from cinematographer to
first mate, skiff driver, skiff mechanic, translator, HD media manager, and production assistant. Corcovado coast, Patagonia, Chile. Photo: Scott Soens
Timmy O'Neill, Corcovado coast, Chile. Photo: Scott Soens

Director of photography Danny Moder (L) and cinematographer Jimmy Chin. (R). Valle Chacabuco, Chile. Photo: Scott Soens

Cinematographer Scott Soens. Valle Chacabuco, Chile. Photo: Scott Soens Collection

Alejandro Navarro (Ramón's father) fishing near Pichilemu. Chile. Photo: Scott Soens

Ramón Navarro at his home near Punta Lobos, Chile. Photo: Scott Soens

The *Cahuelmo* at low tide in a sheltered cove. On the coast below Corcovado, Chile. Photo: Danny Moder

AROUND THE CAMPFIRE

CONVERSATIONS WITH YVON CHOUINARD, JEFF JOHNSON, CHRIS MALLOY, AND DOUG TOMPKINS

THE BLACK CAVE

Chris Malloy: Yvon, take us through the first ascent of the North America Wall in 1964.

Yvon Chouinard: The first ascent was a big breakthrough in American mountaineering. I had been drafted into the Army, and when I came out we put together a group: Tom Frost, myself, Chuck Pratt, and Royal Robbins. We were among the four strongest climbers in America at the time.

The North America Wall is the steepest on El Capitan and one of the few climbs where you can't sit below and follow the route with high-powered binoculars. There were no rescue groups in those days, and only a handful of climbers in the world – guys like Layton Kor – who had the big-wall skills to rescue us. There were no rangers to drop a rope from the top. We were on our own.

I remember being at the base of the climb and getting freaked out. The light was coming down the wall as the sun came up. I saw a falcon way up high; he was just a dot. He takes about four beats of his wings and goes into a two hundred and eighty mile-an-hour dive and then he goes into the dark shadow of the wall and I'm thinking, that's us, but we're going the other way.

We were a really good team. Two of us would climb and two of us would haul. We would switch off every day. It was a big adventure. We really didn't know how we were going to get up there in places.

My parents knew I climbed, but I never bothered to tell them what climbing was and they didn't understand it. They were watching the news on TV one day, and they see these guys up on El Capitan, five days up, in the middle of the wall. We had bivouacked under this huge roof. There's a helicopter shot and all of a sudden it zooms in on these guys hanging in hammocks underneath this great roof and one of them is their son. It suddenly dawned on them what climbing was about.

Chris: Were you in the black cave?

Yvon: Yeah. Yeah. As it turns out, there is a great crack going right out underneath it, but boy it was pretty spooky. Pratt led that. I'd much rather lead it than follow it. To follow it you've got to lower yourself, and you go swinging out over fifteen hundred feet of space. That was pretty weird.

Doing that climb proved that you could climb anything. It proved that there was no wall that was not climbable, and that's when everyone started going to Europe and Baffin Island and doing big walls everywhere.

Jeff Johnson and Yvon Chouinard aboard the *Cahuelmo*. Chaitén, Chile. Photo: Danny Moder

The horse remains the main transportation mode for most Patagonians. Valle Chacabuco, Chile. Photo: Danny Moder

Park rangers round up their supply of extra horses. Valle Chacabuco, Chile. Photo: Danny Moder

Doug Tompkins inside the Hobbit's House. Reñihué, Chile. Photo: Frame-grab from the film *180° South*

MOUNTAIN OF STORMS

Chris Malloy: Doug and Yvon, you wouldn't know this, but about ten years ago Jeff and my brothers and I stumbled on a copy of *Mountain of Storms*, the film you made of your 1968 trip. That movie spoke to us; it changed our take on everything. It really moved us because we just saw how much fun you guys were having – it was raw and not self-important. The film became a compass for us. We watched it, and started to learn more about who you were and what you both had done.

Yvon Chouinard: The trip was Doug's idea; he'd been down there before. We bought this little van and took off from Ventura with surfboards, skis, and climbing gear. You have to remember the Pan-American Highway was pretty wild in 1968. It was a dirt road from Mexico City all the way south, and we had a lot of adventures on that six-month trip. On one morning we woke up with guns pointed at our heads; we were sleeping on the ground outside some little town in Guatemala. Turned out the army was looking for some rebels. The soldiers were sixteen- or seventeen-year-old kids with machine guns; they were nervous and shaking.

Doug Tompkins: They told us an American ambassador had been shot the night before.

Yvon: We surfed all down the coastline of Mexico and El Salvador. We were probably the first guys to surf some of those places. We tried to surf in Costa Rica and a volcano erupted nearby. We were sitting on our boards in the lineup and in about five minutes our whole boards were covered in ashes. Then in Ecuador we met up with a bullfighter, stayed at his family's house.

Doug: We surfed in Panama; we went up the coast north of Panama City. From Panama we went to Colombia by ship, got off in Cartagena, then wound through the mountains of Colombia, down into Quito, then dropped down to the ocean. That's when we went up the coast to Salinas.

Gauchos Erasmo Betancore and Alfonso Ruiz enjoying a conversation during a packing trip. Valle Chacabuco, Chile. Photo: Danny Moder

WITH A MINT ON TOP

Yvon Chouinard: Surfing and climbing are both useless sports. You get to be conquistadors of the useless. You climb to the summit and there is nothing there. You could hike to the top from another direction. It's how you get there that is the important part. It's the same with surfing.

Chris Malloy: Getting back to the '68 trip.

Yvon: It was the best trip of my life. We were already on the path we would follow the rest of our lives, but the trip had a big influence on me. I ended up naming my company after Patagonia, because I wanted to make clothing for conditions down here. You look at the label and it's a stormy sky and mountains and high winds – that's the kind of clothing I wanted to make.

It was a long trip. On short trips you never get into the culture. It's like doing a short climb; you lose a lot. For me, the most fun part of climbing was bivouacking – getting up on a wall and sleeping in god-awful conditions, in hammocks, or just hanging from your ropes all night trying to sleep. You really get into the rhythm of the wall. Climbing El Cap, the first few days you start getting into it; by the eighth or ninth day you feel like you're at home. You start spacing out and looking at the little red bugs on the rock that you never saw before and you calm down completely. You get the sense of being at home. Taking a trip for six months, you get into the rhythm of it. It feels like you could just go on forever.

It's all about the process, not the goal.

Take fly fishing: If you want to catch fish, use a worm. You'll catch so many fish you won't believe it. But fishing with flies takes the same approach as in Zen archery. You don't try to hit the bull's-eye. You concentrate instead on every step you need to take to fire the arrow. It's the same with climbing. If you're climbing a wall in Yosemite, the important thing is how you climb the wall, how you get to the top, because there's no point to just getting to the top.

The opposite of the Zen approach is climbing Everest if you're a plastic surgeon or a CEO. You pay eighty thousand dollars and have sherpas put all the ladders in place and eight thousand feet of fixed rope, and you don't even have to carry a pack. There's a sherpa in front and he's got a three-foot rope on you, and there's a sherpa in back and he's carrying extra oxygen bottles. You get to a camp and you don't even have to lay out your sleeping bag. It's already laid out with a little mint on the top. Your guides have computers dialed into the daily weather report. You bullshit yourself into thinking you climbed Everest, but you didn't climb Everest. You climbed a subdued mountain with all these ropes holding it down, and the whole point of climbing something is a spiritual/physical game. If you compromise the process, and you're an asshole when you start out, then you're an asshole when you get back: Nothing's changed.

Jeff Johnson on the drive south to Valle Chacabuco. Chile. Photo: Danny Moder

WORKING WITH MY HANDS

Yvon Chouinard: I love the rhythm of repetitive movement. I used to blacksmith for hours at a time, eight hours at the forge. I had my fire, and I would grab a piton with my tongs, take one step and go over to my little trip hammer; *bam-bam-bam*. Over to the anvil, straighten it out a little bit. And put it back in the fire. I did that for hours and hours. After about six or eight hours, I would start to trip out. There was an old, rusty barrel there, and I would look at that thing and the rust would just be glowing.

I love working. I've got to work every day with my hands. Even if I am doing paperwork all day, I've got to go home and chop vegetables or something. It's really important to me.

Jeff Johnson: That's what people are losing today, working with their hands. It's that way with everything. Even with photographs now. I hardly ever see a print. It's just in the camera and then in the computer. They show you their family vacation on the computer.

I just switched to digital photography. I was at my grandmother's house recently and found a box of photographs of old cars, old trucks, and people in my family that I didn't know. I didn't know that my grandfather was a boxer. I saw all these shots of him boxing. And I thought about it. I take a lot of photographs and someday my grandkids will say, "Where's Grandpa's hard drive?" There won't be a shoebox laying around with photographs in it. There will just be some hard drive that they won't be able to open. It's kind of sad.

Yvon: That is sad because you lose your history and your culture, and it becomes hard to tell who you are anymore. I have seen that a lot, hanging out with the Indians in the Pacific Northwest. The ones that have lost their culture are really lost. The only ones that seem to be keeping it are the old women. The men are always willing to jump to another culture and absorb the worst of it. The women are hanging on to the old ways. They seem to know.

Yvon Chouinard at his forge. Ventura, California. Photo: Tim Davis

CONQUISTADORS OF THE USELESS

Chris Malloy: I showed you a picture of Corcovado a year and a half ago and you sailed five months to get here, then you hiked forty hours…

Jeff Johnson: Well, that's the hardest part. We put so much time and effort getting there. We had been staring at the mountain for days. To get to the base we had to hike a three-sixty around it. That took three days. And then we got there, and got that summit fever. We wanted it so bad, we worked so hard for it; but we just had to call it off at a certain point.

Sailing here took five months. There is a lot of sitting around on a boat, a lot of down time, a lot of time to think. I had been thinking about that mountain for five months. But that time on the boat also taught me patience. In the end, you just need to be patient and make good decisions; it wasn't easy to walk away from that mountain.

Chris: So twenty years from now, what will you remember most? The climbing, or the sailing, or what you got out of the thinking?

Jeff: I have no idea. Ask me again in twenty years.

Yvon Chouinard: You never know ahead of time what you are going to get out of it.

Jeff: I remember writing in my journal that when you set out on something like this, you know it is going to change something in you, but you don't know what that is. People make a mistake to pinpoint what they want changed in their life, as though they are going out on an adventure to change a certain thing. Then, when it is over they find out they didn't get what they wanted. I think that's where a lot of people go wrong.

Yvon: You get these guys who build a sailboat from scratch. They spend five years doing it. They get it built, and then they don't want to sail anymore. But, what they really wanted was to build a sailboat. That was it.

Our '68 trip was six months long and was a similar thing. Our goal was to do a new route on Fitz Roy, which we did. And we had to do it because we were committed to doing a film on it. But that's not what I remember most about the trip.

There were little incidents: I broke my neck diving off a bridge in Colombia. We were on a bridge over this café au lait water. Doug dives off and says, "Hey, it's great, c'mon." I was standing five feet from him, five feet, and I dove off and hit a sandbar. It cracked my neck and I just lay there. I couldn't move and I am thinking I am paralyzed for the rest of my life. Of course I wasn't. But that led to years of lower back pain, and that led to discovering a tumpline. I went on a forty-six-day trip across the Himalayas, and I saw these porters with tumplines carrying huge loads: hundred-pound loads with tumplines on their heads. And I thought, shit, they are the pros. They are doing it the old way. So I started carrying loads with a tumpline. By the end of the trip, I was carrying fifty pounds, and breaking trail for the sherpas. I have used one ever since.

I'm always trying to find a simple solution rather than a techno fix for everything that I do. So I didn't bring any carabiners on this climb. I tied in with a knot. Instead of putting in anchors to get Makohe down, I would have done the whole thing with just the rope. No carabiners, no slings, no rappel devices. It can all be done really simply. Maybe that's what I got out of breaking my neck on that trip: Do things simply.

Jeff: That's exactly what you got. It's funny what you remember from that trip. I've seen *Mountain of Storms* maybe three or four times. And I don't even remember seeing the summit. What I remember is just you guys surfing, skiing, goofing off. I hardly remember the Fitz Roy part. Getting there is the coolest part of the film, I thought.

And this trip, I didn't even care about the summit. I wanted to climb the thing really bad, but as soon as I knew it was too dangerous, I didn't care. Who cares?

Yvon: Conquistadors of the useless.

Jeff: Just like you said: Climbing is totally useless.

Yvon: But it's a great goal.

Jeff: It is a great goal. And like you, I've always used climbing and surfing as an excuse to see all these places. I used to get in these conversations with my mom. I would go to these countries and she would ask me, "Did you see this? Did you see that?" And I'd say, "No I didn't see any of that." "Well what the hell did you do?" she would ask. And I would reply, "I went surfing and I hung out in this one town for a month." She'd say, "I can't believe you are going to these places and you are not seeing things like the Eiffel Tower or the Coliseum." And I go, "Well I stayed with a local family, and drank beer at the local bar, and hung out for a month and surfed." If it wasn't for surfing, I wouldn't be in these funky little towns hanging out with these people.

Yvon: I'll tell you what happened to Doug and me one time when we went to Uganda. I've always loved those great nineteenth-century explorer books – you know, Burton and Speke, and Livingston and Stanley – they were always looking for the source of the Nile. They figured the source of the Nile was Lake Victoria, but then Lake Albert drains into Lake Victoria, and then the stream that fills Lake Albert comes out of the Ruwenzori Range, the Mountains of the Moon. Anyway, the highest peak there is Mount Stanley. Doug and I stood on the top of Stanley and took a piss. For a brief moment in time we were the source of the Nile.

That's useless, right? If somebody asked, "Why did you climb Mount Stanley?" we would have answered, "So we could be the source of the Nile." That's as good an answer as any.

Chris: Yvon, what's the difference between success and failure when it comes to climbing?

Yvon: What's important is the effort. We put in a lot of effort on Corcovado. I mean, three days of just trying to get there. If it's important that we climbed it, made a second ascent, and wrote it up for history books, then we failed. But if we were out for a good adventure, then we were successful.

Chris: What's your idea of success and failure in life?

Yvon: There was a book I liked called *Epitaph of a Small Winner*. The guy assesses his life and tries to decide whether he is a winner or a loser. And it turns out he is a small winner.

It's different for everyone. I guess it depends what is important to you. For me, trying this climb was great because I could see, at almost seventy years old, how far I could push myself. My mind was fine. I wasn't caving in. But my body didn't follow too well.

Over my life, I have pushed myself. I know how far I can go in the cold and heat, and I know I can feed my family from the ocean. I know I can drink from trout streams. It gives me confidence.

Rodrigo Noriega in his Cessna. Cerro Corcavado, Chile. Photo: Jeff Johnson

The proposed site, near the entrance of Valle Chacabuco, of one of two hydroelectric dams to go on the Rio Baker. The Baker is the largest wild, free-flowing river in Chilean Patagonia. An additional three dams are planned for the nearby Pascua River. The dams are to supply electricity to big cities, which means bulldozing a strip to run high-tension wires all the way up the length of the Patagonian Andes to Santiago. The rural people from the region are skeptical of the promise that this project will improve their lives.

The residents surrounding the Bio Bio had similar promises that were never lived up to when their river was dammed a decade ago. Patagonia, Chile. Photo: Scott Soens

ON SPIRITUALITY

Chris Malloy: People might call you doomsdayers, but look at what you've built. Walk out of this cabin and look around; you're fighting to the bitter end for change.

Doug Tompkins: Well, you can be a doomsdayer and fight.

Yvon Chouinard: Absolutely, I'm a doomsdayer. We are all going to die – some people don't accept that fact. You're going to die, but that doesn't mean you give up. Everything has a beginning and an end. Society has a beginning and an end. Every culture has a beginning and an end. Every species has a beginning and an end. We are going to have an end. But you don't want to be part of the cause of accelerating it. You want to live your life so that you're part of the solution and not the cause.

Doug: First, we might be mistaken. Maybe we are doing it all wrong. Maybe we have the wrong take on everything. Maybe the techno-industrialists are right. Maybe they are going to come up with one technological fix after the other.

Chris: Do you mean that?

Doug: I leave it open as a possibility. I don't think it's true, but on the other hand I think it would be dogmatic and dangerous to think we have all the answers, because we don't.

Yvon: It's like asking whether there is a God or not. How do you know one way or another?

Chris: It's interesting you say that, because you come across as this sort of unspiritual person.

Yvon: I'm very spiritual. I believe there are lives in rocks because rocks have movement, atoms bouncing around each other. Rocks are alive. Having that belief, it doesn't interest me to drill another bolt, or put another hole in a rock.

Chris: Yesterday Makohe caught a fish and according to her, the energy in the river goes into the fish, and when we catch the fish and eat it, the energy of the river is transferred to us. There is a spiritual side to leaving places alone.

Yvon: Makohe has a really good concept of that; she has lived a life very close to nature. She tells the story of when she was young and living on Easter Island, she wanted to go to Chile because she heard fish came in packages in plastic wrap and that was the most curious thing. She couldn't believe that could happen. For most kids now it would be weird to go out and actually catch a fish and kill it. Most of them wouldn't have the guts to kill it, clean it, and cook it. They are so divorced from that. People won't even drink water unless it comes in a bottle.

Yvon Chouinard and Doug Tompkins inside the Hobbit's House. Reñihué, Chile. Photo: Frame-grab from the film *180° South*

THERE'S A SHIFT HERE

Chris Malloy: I hate to break it to you, but a lot of people think you guys are nuts.

Doug Tompkins: That's not the first time we've heard that.

Chris: I sense that you guys are ruining their paradigm. I can see all the CEOs saying, "Goddamn, Chouinard, I'm going to have to change my whole money-making project." Or you, Doug, you've got people in Santiago who own vast tracts of land down in Patagonia and haven't been down here in two generations, and they don't want to change the way they manage their land.

When news about what you two are doing comes out and people start attacking you, do you care about those people? Do you give a shit? Do you ignore them? Do you want to learn more about them so you know who your enemies are? Do you consider them enemies?

Yvon Chouinard: Well, I've got a lot fewer enemies than Doug does. I don't have much hassle with that. But, Doug is down here in a society where there is no such thing as philanthropy. Most of these wealthy families in Latin America made their money through devious means, and they are not about to give it away.

The whole history of Latin America is conquistadors coming down, killing off the Indians, stealing the wealth; it's the history of manifest destiny. It's not much different from the States, but in the States at least we don't trust the government to do good, so we have a history of philanthropy. There are a million NGOs in America; there are thirty thousand environmental organizations trying to do good work.

But there's no history of philanthropy in Latin America. So Doug comes down here and buys up all this land and starts to create a national park and says, "I'm going to give the land back to you Chileans or Argentineans." And they reply, "Give me a break. People don't do that; there has to be another reason." There are all these wise-use guys down here that believe that taking land off the tax rolls hurts the country, and there has got to be another reason. So Doug has been attacked and vilified. I don't have to deal with that in my own life, but it's a different story for him.

Doug: Now that I've been here for eighteen years, people have come to know what we are doing and a lot of people have come to understand our point of view. We have conservation projects in Chile, and local activists and NGOs dealing with specific issues like agriculture, dams and rivers, irresponsible road building. People have come around – not everybody of course, but a lot of people now understand our work. You still can get the powers that be against you for your view of the world – the military, sometimes the church, even the political class, and certainly part of the entrepreneurial class.

Over the years I've become more outspoken. Opposition to conservation thrust us into the public eye, and in a way gave us the microphone. Once you get the microphone, you can speak to a broader public about your ideas for conservation. There are a lot more Chileans, more every day, joining our side as part of a worldwide movement towards conservation.

There is a shift here, as there is in every society, and I think it's unstoppable. The environmental crisis is getting sharper and deeper. The crisis itself is pushing society as a whole to face these real problems over water, air, soil erosion, ocean biomass, and forest cover.

A small farm in Horno Perrin. Patagonia, Chile. Photo: Frame-grab from the film *180° South*

CAN'T IMPROVE ON NATURE

Chris Malloy: Yvon, do you feel the planet is sort of screwed no matter what?

Yvon Chouinard: Yeah, the planet is screwed no matter what. For me, being around this long and traveling – I've done climbs on every continent, gone all around the world – I see nothing but deterioration. That doesn't mean that you give up. It means you do what you can, but you have a realistic view that this is the way it is.

For me, humans are like any other mammal. What is important is trying to save as many species, including people, as possible. I like the whole idea of diversity. I believe in nature, and I think nature loves diversity. That's why it made so many species. And humans are eliminating them as fast as we can. It just isn't right.

You can't improve on nature. We are trying with genetic modification to engineer better crops. In the end, this whole green revolution has been done with petrochemicals. We are losing topsoil at a rate of an inch a year. We are making foods that have seventy percent less nutrients. So what did we accomplish? We made *more* food, but in the end we are still starving.

Take an organic garden, and you can produce almost as much food as you can with industrial agriculture. Yet the food is much more nutritious, tastes better, and builds soil instead of destroying it. Without petrochemicals this whole green revolution thing falls apart.

Gaucho Alfonso Ruiz enjoying some down time during a packing trip. Valle Chacabuco, Chile. Photo: Jeff Johnson

Gaucho Eduardo Castro at Casa de Piedra taking a maté break. Valle Chacabuco, Chile. Photo: Jeff Johnson

TURN AROUND AND TAKE A FORWARD STEP

Chris Malloy: How would you guys describe each other?

Yvon Chouinard: We are opposites. If you look around here, you'll see little carvings everywhere. Doug approved every single one of them. I don't have the energy to do that stuff.

He is more bothered about the end of society and the end of mankind than I am, because he wants to do something about it and stop it. I'm just a laid-back Zen Buddhist about it. I say, wow, I'll do what I can and so be it. We have the same view of the world and where it's going, but a different approach.

Doug Tompkins: I tell Yvon that a good Buddhist has to take his Bodhisattva vows: that before you reach self-enlightenment you have to end the suffering of the world. I'm not so concerned about where human society is going; it seems pretty clear where it's going. I'm more concerned about nonhuman society and the demise of nature itself.

We are going to have to rethink the economic model. We have to rethink capitalism. Of course, the moment you say "you have to rethink capitalism," then everyone says, "Oh, now we are going to have communism!" But that is hardly the only way to examine our economic model. And if we examine, if we deconstruct, our economic model, we discover that free-market capitalism is thrusting us into the abyss of history. We need to think about pulling back from the edge of that abyss if we possibly can – if it's not too late to do that.

I keep coming back to those five major indicators of the health of our environment: water, air, soil, biomass in the ocean, and forest cover. All those indicators are trending down. That would make one think it's worth examining, in a systematic way, what kind of bloody economic model we are following.

We need to really change, not just reform, the system. If you buy a Prius you lessen your impact, but you continue to promote and perpetuate the car culture, which is where the problem lies. People say, "I can't imagine a world without cars, how are we going to get around, how's this all going to work?" That's just a lack of imagination. As my buddy Jim Kunstler says, the greatest obstacle in our collective imagination today is our obsession to keep the cars running by other means. If they are not going to run on gas and oil, we'll run them on electricity, or hydrogen, or methane, or ethanol. But we will still have the car culture, which means we will still have roads, and we will have fragmented habitats, and we will expand, and expand, and expand the human project until we fall off the edge.

As I see it, that's the dilemma of social movements focused on the future and the plight of our planet. We have to go far beyond thinking that we can simply reform the system. I know this is revolutionary talk, but there is going to have to be some kind of revolution to change our current direction.

Yvon: Maintaining the car culture is the classic example: There is no right way to do the wrong thing. It's impossible. David Brower used to say the solution to a lot of the world's problems requires you to turn around and take a forward step. You can't just try to make a flawed system work.

Yvon Chouinard outside Casa de Piedra. Valle Chacabuco, Chile. Photo: Frame-grab from the film *180° South*

Kitchen/living room at Casa de Piedra, a bunkhouse-turned-pack station for the gauchos who have become park rangers. Valle Chacabuco, Chile. Photo: Jeff Johnson

Bedroom at Casa de Piedra. Valle Chacabuco, Chile. Photo: Jeff Johnson

Doug Tompkins flies over Reñihué in his Husky A-1. Patagonia, Chile. Photo: Scott Soens

NATURE AND TECHNOLOGY

Chris Malloy: How has John Muir's legacy affected you?

Doug Tompkins: If you look around the world in the last hundred years at who launched the ideas taken up by others, John Muir was definitely a major figure. He was an outdoor person who loved nature for nature's sake. He didn't see the world in terms of utilitarian productivity – a more-or-less Western worldview, which sees nature as a basket of resources, a cornucopia to benefit the human economy.

Of course, the human economy does use resources, but Muir saw the value of nature in itself; that there is intrinsic worth to not just the mountains, or a species, but for nature in its entirety. His philosophical perspective informed generations that came after him and, in many ways, he is the father of the American conservation movement.

Once you go along with the concept of nature having intrinsic value, you take different strategies to create policy change. Muir also was a kindred spirit to the relatively small circle of people in our generation who loved the outdoors. Certainly, I was influenced by Muir and his writings. He was seminal to conservationists and activists like Dave Foreman and David Brower.

Yvon Chouinard: Muir influenced us a lot, Muir and the naturalist American philosophers, Emerson and Thoreau.

My climbing heroes were all Europeans – all the north-wall climbers in the Alps. The Europeans had a manifest-destiny philosophy as far as climbing goes. They were conquering the mountains – they'd do a new route and leave all the pitons in place to make it easier for mankind to follow.

Our attitude was to do these climbs and leave no trace. That got me into the business of hammering out pitons, a better piton – made of steel rather than iron – that could be used over and over again instead of just once. Reusable pitons allowed us to do these big walls on El Capitan.

But for every technology there is an unintended consequence. So many climbers putting in these pitons and taking them out started to scar the rock on the popular routes. And I thought, I've created this technology that is actually ruining the thing I love. So we got away from using pitons and into using these little chocks you could jam in with your fingers and slip out without using a hammer. That was a good lesson. It taught me that you've really got to lead an examined life. You've got to be careful adopting any new technology because you never know what the unintended consequences of that technology are going to be.

Doug: Of course the promoters of the new technology never tell you about that. I remember talking to Steve Jobs about personal computers ruining the world. For him the benefits are unarguable – and it is pretty hard to argue against some of the benefits computers provide. The trouble is that computers have an overwhelmingly negative influence. They accelerate economic activity and the transfer of nature to the realm of production. That means less biomass in the ocean, less forest cover, more soil erosion, more contaminated water, and the building up of what's called a phantom carrying capacity.

This is not the sort of thing Apple wants to advertise – it's against their self-interest. It takes a very special businessperson to say we are making something that is good for our business, but bad for the world. Every once in a while someone does something like change from pitons to chocks, but that's rare. Mostly technology just keeps marching forward, and the world just gets poorer and poorer for it.

Yvon: Modern man thinks we can do without nature, or we're better than nature. We can manipulate it in our own way. We don't need free-flowing rivers to have salmon: we can farm them. But Muir and these other philosophers said that we are part of nature, that we can't divorce ourselves from it.

We are going through the sixth mass extinction of species around the world – and we are a species. Somehow we think we're not going to be part of that extinction. But in fact, as one of the big mammals, we'll probably go first. The key to any kind of so-called sustainability is to take care of nature, to work with nature. To think we're better than nature – and can come up with something to isolate us from the laws of nature – is ridiculous.

Doug: Indigenous cultures all over the world have a cosmological vision. They believed that we were part of a great system. That great system is what modern society calls ecology. Everything is connected with everything else. As long as we base our economy on the technological worldview, not the ecological worldview, we are going to continue to take society – global society – into the abyss.

Five hydroelectric dams are planned for construction along the Baker and Pascua rivers in southern Chile. Most of the local residents oppose the dams because their livelihoods depend on free-flowing rivers. Up in arms, gaucho Erasmo Betancore set out on horseback for a four-day ride to protest at the capital. Word got out as he passed the small ranches and farms along the way. Within two days more than 200 riders had joined him; by the time they reached the capital that number had grown to more than 300. Photo: Frame-grab from the film *180° South*

Jeff Johnson on his drive to Valle Chacabuco passes one of the many "¡Sin Represas!" (Without Dams) banners. Photo: Frame-grab from the film *180° South*

More than 300 riders make the journey to the capital to protest against the dams along the Baker and Pascua rivers. Patagonia, Chile. Photo: Frame-grab from the film *180° South*
Following spread: Valle Chacabuco, Chile. Photo: Scott Soens